STUDENT UNIT GUIDE

NEW EDITION

Edexcel AS Business Studies
Economics & Business Unit 1

Developing New Business Ideas

Brian Ellis

Philip Allan Updates, an imprint of Hodder Education, an Hachette UK company, Market Place, Deddington, Oxfordshire OX15 0SE

Orders

Bookpoint Ltd, 130 Milton Park, Abingdon, Oxfordshire OX14 4SB

tel: 01235 827827

fax: 01235 400401

e-mail: education@bookpoint.co.uk

Lines are open 9.00 a.m.–5.00 p.m., Monday to Saturday, with a 24-hour message answering service. You can also order through the Philip Allan Updates website: www.philipallan.co.uk

© Brian Ellis 2011

ISBN 978-1-4441-4794-0

First printed 2011
Impression number 5 4 3 2
Year 2015 2014 2013 2012

Cover photo: Akio Koizumi/Fotolia

Printed in Dubai

Hachette UK's policy is to use papers that are natural, renewable and recyclable products and made from wood grown in sustainable forests. The logging and manufacturing processes are expected to conform to the environmental regulations of the country of origin.

P01917

Contents

Content Guidance

Questions & Answers

Getting the most from this book

Examiner tips

Advice from the examiner on key points in the text to help you learn and recall unit content, avoid pitfalls, and polish your exam technique in order to boost your grade.

Knowledge check

Rapid-fire questions throughout the Content Guidance section to check your understanding.

Knowledge check answers

1 Turn to the back of the book for the Knowledge check answers.

Summary

Summaries

● Each core topic is rounded off by a bullet-list summary for quick-check reference of what you need to know.

Questions & Answers

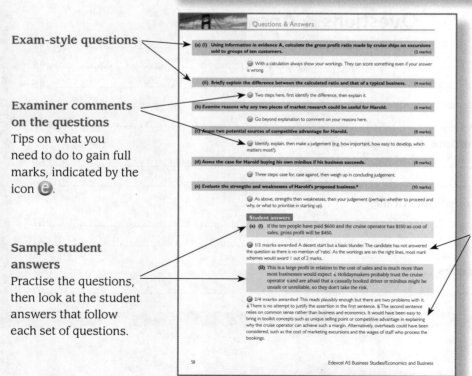

Exam-style questions

Examiner comments on the questions
Tips on what you need to do to gain full marks, indicated by the icon **e**.

Sample student answers
Practise the questions, then look at the student answers that follow each set of questions.

Examiner commentary on sample student answers
Find out how many marks each answer would be awarded in the exam and then read the examiner comments (preceded by the icon **e**) following each student answer. Annotations that link back to points made in the student answers show exactly how and where marks are gained or lost.

About this book

The main aim of this guide is to help you prepare successfully for the Edexcel examination in 'Developing New Business Ideas'. This is the first AS unit for students taking either Business Studies or the combined Economics and Business course. It represents half an AS course or a quarter of an A-level.

The skills needed to do well in this unit are valuable in both business and economics. A key aim of both this book and the course is to help prepare decision makers for the future business world. Besides aims of developing interest, enthusiasm and understanding, the course targets the ability to 'generate enterprising and creative solutions to business problems and issues'. It will help if you are willing to think out your own opinions and explain your justification for them — and not expect simply to be told all the right answers. The Edexcel specification has a unique blend of the academic with the practical, which is reflected in this guide.

This guide is not a traditional textbook; it is more sharply focused on preparation for the exam. You might find it particularly valuable as you revise, but it can also assist in your learning and development of ideas throughout study of the unit.

The **Content Guidance** section gives an overview of topics covered in the unit. Concepts and theories are a **toolkit** in this course, equipment for tackling problems and for understanding issues in Business and Economics. Examples are included in this guide but it is always sensible to think about additional situations in which any concept might be relevant and useful.

The sections on assessment objectives and exam format are as important as anything else in this guide. There are students who are locked into the idea that exams test knowledge, that learning and reproducing 'facts' in exams is enough. This is simply not true: knowledge and understanding can earn just 21 of the 70 marks available in exams for this unit. Getting to grips with and developing the higher skills is probably more valuable than any piece of content learning.

The **Question and Answer** section gives examples in the styles you can expect from live exam papers, with both supported multiple-choice and structured data–response questions. The sample answers plus examiner comments show you both some mistakes to avoid and some effective approaches to adopt.

Key terms are highlighted in green and are briefly defined in the margin as they arise.

These sections are not designed to be of equal length. For example, the section on 'Evaluating a business' has more content so can be expected to be the basis for more exam questions. Not surprisingly, it is also given more space in this guide.

Characteristics of successful entrepreneurs

What does it take?

What is an entrepreneur?

The image that some young people have of business organisers is generally of much older individuals who are different from them. Examples that spring to mind most easily are probably 'celebrities' such as Richard Branson, figurehead of the Virgin Group, Alan Sugar who seems to spend considerable time appearing on television, or Anita Roddick who founded and developed The Body Shop.

There are more businesses (and business organisers) around than you might guess. For example, around 3.5 million self-employed people in the UK (source: **www.statistics.gov.uk**, September 2007) all technically run their own business. In areas such as computer games and internet applications there have been thriving businesses run by people not yet old enough to leave school. Many people, young and old, have the potential to run a successful business but underestimate themselves or shy away from taking responsibility and action.

What are the characteristics of an entrepreneur?

We use the term entrepreneur to refer to anyone who organises and runs a business. Some characteristics are probably essential in an entrepreneur and others are useful. Most entrepreneurs are stronger on some characteristics than on others.

Risk taking

First of all, there is an element of risk in running any business. This risk should be considered and can be minimised but it is an inescapable feature of business. What if an idea that is turned into a business fails to attract customers? What if a rival business comes up with a better and cheaper version of your product? As in life, it is impossible to eliminate risk from business. Lightning can strike anywhere. If you ride a bike on a road you risk being struck by a careless driver. Entrepreneurs should not be careless, but they must accept some risk. A great many actions and activities carry an element of risk. Some people are risk averse and as careful as possible; some 'chancers' take risks that most of us find unacceptable. An entrepreneur cannot avoid all business risk and must be able to cope with it.

entrepreneur someone who takes responsibility for organising business activity and carries business risk.

Knowledge check 1

Why might risk-averse people not make good entrepreneurs?

risk averse reluctant to take any chances, probably not an entrepreneur.

Time and energy

Running a business takes time and energy. Professional **managers** can be brought into an established business if it generates sufficient income, but the development of a new business is hard work. This means that willingness to work is important. Running a business can fill almost all the waking hours of some entrepreneurs and effectively take over their lives. This is clearly more acceptable if they are energetic and enjoy the business activity. From another perspective we can say that some people like to stay in their 'comfort zone' and not stretch or test their abilities; others like a challenge and enjoy problem solving. Entrepreneurs are normally drawn from this second, more proactive, personality type.

managers the people who organise and control a business. Managers typically have both power and responsibility.

Initiative

A new business requires initiative, readiness to come up with ideas, make decisions and take action. Dithering or too frequently changing a business strategy creates problems, as does an ineffective approach. If the going gets tough, some people give up whereas others are resolute. There will normally be disappointments and problems in starting a business, so self-confidence, determination and the resilience to keep on going despite obstacles are also valuable characteristics of an entrepreneur. If you do not trust your own judgement and are easily put off when others do not share your views, you will struggle to run a business. At the same time, you must be willing to acknowledge mistakes and ready to put things right if they go wrong.

Creative skills

Having flair or a talent for design and presentation of the product can frequently make an important difference. Creative skills are valuable in the context of many businesses; how important depends on the nature of the product and the ways in which customers are attracted. There is a clear contrast between people whose priority is to run a successful business, choosing whatever seems most likely to be profitable, and others whose enthusiasm draws them to a particular product or industry.

Examiner tip
Creative skills matter far more in some business types than others. Stressing the characteristics relevant to the business in a question shows good 'application'.

Interpersonal and communication skills

Other characteristics and skills that can be valuable include interpersonal and communication skills (e.g. to sell the product and/or to keep up employee motivation), numeracy (to keep track of money and of how the business is progressing) and IT skills as computers are useful tools for most businesses. Once we move into skills rather than natural characteristics, there is the advantage that they can definitely be improved via training. Education and training can do much to equip future entrepreneurs but some 'natural' characteristics are hard to learn. Skills can also be 'bought in' once a business can afford this — many entrepreneurs are pleased to pass keeping financial records to an accountant, for example.

Strengths and weaknesses

Do you think the characteristics and skills of entrepreneurs listed above are in the order of their importance? Are there characteristics that you would move higher up the list or other qualities that you see as important that should be added? Are some characteristics important enough that strength in them can make up for weaknesses in other areas?

If we look at local entrepreneurs or national 'celebrity' business people, we will see that they are not all identical. Some seem to succeed despite lacking one or more of the valuable characteristics. If they have significant weaknesses, perhaps these can sometimes be outweighed by great strengths in other directions. The same thing is true in sport or in teaching. People with great strengths can excel despite some weaknesses.

Motivation: why do it?

motivation the reasons (or impulses) that lead us to act as we do.

manufacturing turning physical inputs into a saleable product; a sector that takes up a falling share of UK business activity.

Motivation can be complicated but can also be simple. Some entrepreneurs prize the independence and responsibility of having control, making their own decisions and handling the consequences. Others enjoy either their finished product or the **manufacturing** or creative processes involved, and want to work with something they love. Motorcycles, animals, the environment or even self-expression are examples of areas of interest that inspire some entrepreneurs.

Other responsibilities

Other priorities might make running a business attractive: for example, a carer committed to looking after children or an elderly parent might set up a business so that they can work from home or work at convenient hours. Becoming the boss helps such people avoid the set hours required by most employers. Someone deeply committed to their local community might start a business in order to provide jobs for themselves and for others in the area. When charities organise their activities they become businesses with the main objective of promoting their cause. Some people place a high value on the independence and self-reliance involved in running their own business.

profit revenue minus costs. Profit can be seen as the reward for enterprise and for carrying business risk.

profit maximisation running a business to make the most profit possible, regardless of any other objectives.

revenue income received by a business from sales and any other sources.

costs the expenditure incurred to operate any business activity.

welfare wellbeing, sometimes measured just in terms of material goods but sometimes taking a wider view of the quality of life.

Profit

One measure of business success is **profit** and the prospect of growing rich from profits has a powerful attraction for some people. A large amount of economic theory starts from the premise that people are **profit maximisers** who set out to generate the highest income possible. As entrepreneurs they focus on generating as much surplus of **revenue** over **costs** as they can. Some theories suggest that profit-maximising, selfish capitalists will work to satisfy customers' desires in order to maximise revenue. In the process they can use resources in such a way that total output and 'welfare' are maximised. You may like to consider if this is realistic in a country where more health problems and deaths are caused by overeating than by undereating.

Even though a charity is primarily motivated by its cause, its survival will depend on raising enough to pay the bills. It cannot ignore the balance between revenue and expenditure. A profit from revenue that is greater than spending will be attractive, as it will enable the charity to do more in future.

Satisficers

Other theories challenge the profit-maximising approach. Many psychologists suggest that anyone motivated only by selfish capitalist ambition is unlikely to have a fully rounded personality and risks a possibility of future mental health problems. 'Satisficers' are people who target a reasonable performance rather than pushing hard for maximum success, and perhaps also look for comfort and relaxation alongside income.

In reality, different businesses and entrepreneurs have various mixed motives. If an interest in the product is combined with enjoying responsibility and generating reasonable income, this will satisfy some entrepreneurs. Just as for employees, we could probably divide entrepreneurs between those who enjoy their work and those who put up with it for the rewards. Those who can enjoy what they do have significant advantages over others for whom their work is just a means to generate income.

Ethics

Motivation can also have an ethical dimension. Some entrepreneurs want to feel both that they are producing something useful for the community and that they are treating staff, suppliers and customers well. Prioritising profit might lead to less interest in, say, other people or the environment. Sourcing low-cost supplies from 'sweatshops' where workers have low wages and poor working conditions, for example, might be profitable but is ethically dubious.

Several large businesses have found that adverse publicity about dubious practices can eat away at profitability. This means that an image of 'corporate responsibility' has become an asset: for example, Global Exchange and other pressure groups forced Nike to change some of its attitudes to suppliers. If you are interested in looking further at Nike as a case study, www.nikebiz.com and the company's own website www.nike.com offer contrasting views.

While some entrepreneurs build a healthy image by insisting on responsible behaviour, others might take a more cynical approach, which sees responsibility as a public relations exercise more than a guide to acceptable conduct. When public relations specialists defend company actions, there are often clues as to whether they are truly ethical or simply applying a superficial ethical gloss. In late 2007 Cadbury Schweppes was attracting criticism for closing UK factories while expanding elsewhere. Whenever you read this guide, there will be current examples of business ethics or ethical failures attracting attention.

Personal objectives

Some possible objectives are listed below in alphabetical order. Rewrite the list in order of their priority for you, leaving out any with no appeal to you. What does your list say about you?

- comfort and relaxation
- convenient hours
- independence
- creativity
- ethical behaviour
- job satisfaction
- profit

satisficers people who target a satisfactory (and perhaps comfortable) performance rather than profit maximisation.

Knowledge check 2
How might you recognise A-level students who are satisficers?

ethical in line with ideas on what is morally correct. Sometimes businesses face a choice between profit maximisation and ethical behaviour.

corporate responsibility businesses taking into account fairness and consideration towards their stakeholders; behaving ethically.

Leadership styles

Autocratic

In any business with employees, managing them involves **leadership**. Some entrepreneurs operate with an **autocratic** style, which entails strict discipline and giving orders that are to be obeyed without question because employees either respect or fear their leader. This type of leadership was seen as normal a century ago and can be effective where it is important to have instructions followed accurately and quickly, for example a platoon of soldiers in combat needs discipline and clear direction. It can be less effective where fresh ideas, flexibility and having proactive staff are valued.

Paternalistic

Employees are seen as a key **asset** in many businesses and one consequence of this can be the use of **paternalistic leadership**, where the entrepreneur still has authority and takes decisions but also takes a kindly and supportive approach to employees. Whereas an autocratic leader might say 'like it or lump it', a paternalistic leader is more likely to say 'please' and 'thank you' while asking/telling people what to do. The contrast here is partly about style — both autocratic and paternalistic leaders retain authority and expect to get their way.

The difference is that paternalistic leaders consider the welfare of employees in reaching decisions, not just profit. This can win loyalty and motivate employees, improving their performance at work. Lee Kwan Yew, a former prime minister of Singapore, once said: 'We decide what is right. Never mind what the people think.' Despite this, he probably thought of himself as paternalistic rather than autocratic.

Democratic

A **democratic** leader involves employees in formulating strategy and making choices, consulting to gather views but still ultimately taking decisions and responsibility. This has two advantages. One is that employees might produce ideas that are better than those the leader could come up with alone. The second is that the employees of a democratic leader are more likely to feel respected, valued and motivated. However, two disadvantages of this approach are that reaching decisions will take more time and that care is necessary to ensure that decisions stay coherent and consistent with the aims and strategy of the organisation. Good democratic leaders have vision and purpose: they are generally not weak. Weak leaders tend to lack the courage to '**empower**' employees. Such people tend to look for scapegoats to blame when things go wrong, creating tension, insecurity and reluctance to take responsibility.

Laissez-faire

It is possible to use *laissez-faire* leadership where employees are left to do things in their own way. The nature of the business is significant here. Where specialist

---

leadership taking responsibility for decisions plus organising and motivating fellow workers.

autocratic means that decisions are handed down for implementation, and subordinates are not expected to question decisions or to offer alternatives.

Examiner tip
Points of view vary. Some leaders who see themselves as democratic are considered autocratic by their employees.

assets things that are useful or valuable are assets. Premises, equipment and goodwill are examples of business assets.

paternalistic leadership where a leader is firmly in control but takes into account workers' welfare.

democratic means leaders consult widely and share decision taking.

empower to assign or delegate freedom, decision taking and responsibility to individuals or teams of employees.

laissez-faire subordinates are allowed as much independence as possible.

labour is involved in a linked sequence of stages of production, careful coordination is necessary and leaders need to set out clear expectations. By contrast, where creative professionals work largely independently, there is a strong case for letting each of them work in their own way: for example, they might choose their own working hours. Besides the nature of the work, the nature of the particular group of employees and the size of the business are also significant. What works well in a small hairdressing salon might not be good for a **multinational** business trying to promote a global image. What works well with an A-level group might bring chaos in Year 9.

Douglas McGregor introduced a basic division which has stood the test of time as an insight on leadership. He contrasted 'Theory X' managers who treated employees as lazy, untrustworthy and needing close supervision with 'Theory Y' managers who saw people as wanting to contribute and work hard if conditions were right for them. Leaders who tend towards the Theory X view will probably see a need for strong, authoritarian leadership. Those inclined towards Theory Y will want to create a positive working environment for their employees and to share responsibility with them.

multinational company/corporation (MNC) a business with activities in several countries. Multinationals (also called transnationals) were once rare but in the twenty-first century there are more than 50,000 of them. They are estimated to control more than a third of global output.

Theory X a management approach based on the idea that people are lazy and need close supervision.

Theory Y a management approach based on the idea that people want to achieve and can be trusted.

Characteristics of successful entrepreneurs

- Useful characteristics for entrepreneurs include readiness to take some risk, energy, initiative, creative skills and interpersonal skills. It is not essential, though, for all entrepreneurs to be strong in all these areas.
- Human motivation is complicated. We sometimes simplify this by assuming that entrepreneurs seek maximum profits, but this underestimates the range and variations of real motives.

Table 1 Features of some major leadership styles

Autocratic	The boss takes decisions and criticism is unwelcome.
Paternalistic	The boss takes decisions and looks after his/her staff.
Democratic	Views are sought before the boss takes responsibility.
Laissez-faire	Maximum independence/responsibility for each worker.

Summary

Identifying a business opportunity

What makes a market?

A **market** is a system that allows buyers and sellers to agree prices and to trade. eBay and call centres show that a market need not necessarily entail a physical location where traders meet, but there are still many retail shops, wholesale markets and exchanges providing the service of bringing buyers and sellers together in person. Technological developments stimulate changes: for example, the London Stock Exchange, where shares are traded, gave up its trading floor where buyers and sellers met to shift to electronic dealing.

market any way of enabling buyers and sellers to trade.

Businesses earn revenue (income) by selling their products or services. This means they have to have a product that customers are willing to buy. Rather than concentrate on the quality and technical excellence of the product, it makes sense to give priority to ensuring that the product matches customers' wishes as closely as possible and is priced attractively. In jargon terms, this means being '**market orientated**' rather than '**product orientated**'. So, for example, a **unique selling point** (USP) — something attractive to buyers and not matched by competitors – is useful.

Another approach is to think in terms of 'competitive advantage', anything which gives an edge over rivals. The emphasis on market orientation has seen firms increasingly sub-contracting or **outsourcing** either components or entire products and concentrating their own efforts on marketing rather than producing. Amstrad, run by Alan Sugar, is a good example of a business taking this approach.

Identifying an interesting market is only the first step for a start-up business. It is necessary to understand the market in terms of its demand, supply and pricing. How much **differentiation** and **segmentation** is there? Are there relatively neglected **market niches**?

Market differentiation

Market differentiation can be achieved by building a strong brand and brand image. Biros and Hoovers are brands that became synonymous with products. Competitive advantage can centre on a cost and price advantage (from **efficiency** or cheap inputs) or on any other way of standing out. One shoe retailer, for example, could focus on sourcing from the cheapest suppliers and charging low prices, while another could specialise in the most up-to-date and fashionable designs. A third retailer might seek competitive advantage by stocking the best-known brand names, while a fourth might pick a location, say in London's Oxford Street, in which many shoppers are found.

Market niche

Shoes might not always be essential but most people see them as a necessity. For products and services that are not essential, initial production and marketing are more risky. Can people be persuaded to want the product? When mobile phones were first introduced it was necessary to persuade people that they would be useful. Once this became established, producers saw one route to competitive advantage in adding functions such as cameras, music players and internet access to their phones — while also minimising their size. The increasing complexity of handsets opened up a market niche (specialised sub-market) for basic, simple phones, with large buttons, to meet the preferences of people who are timid about complicated technology.

Market demand

A market will grow if there is sufficient demand (desire backed by readiness to pay) to make supplying the item profitable. High profits will attract more producers. Mobile phones have an almost global appeal; both demand and supply have grown rapidly. Most high streets have a choice of mobile phone suppliers; there are also mail order and internet options. Pricing in this market is complex because network operators will subsidise handsets in return for profitable monthly contracts but there is also the option of pay-as-you-go.

The situation in business is not static. At any time, there will be expanding markets (like mobile phones), fairly stable markets (like men's clothing) and shrinking markets (video hire has suffered from a switch to DVDs and recently from the growth of internet downloads). Business parks and high streets reflect the fortunes of different markets over time. An expanding market has obvious attractions but other entrepreneurs will be attracted too. To break into a stable market successfully requires an effective source of competitive advantage. This probably entails a good USP or a deliberate plan to compete by avoiding the weaknesses identified in competitors. Sometimes a new technology will open a route to better products. When others exit from a declining market they can leave gaps which are at least profitable in the short term: for example, those shoe repair shops that are left can charge high prices.

Demand

Demand, sometimes called **effective demand**, is our measure of how much of a product or service **consumers** actually buy in a market. For example, the demand for motor cars in the UK is about 2–3 million a year. The influences of several factors combine to determine the level of demand.

Population structure

Population is an important determinant of demand. The **population structure** matters too. Britain has an ageing population with an increasing number and proportion of pensioners, so the senior citizen market is expanding, which means, for example, that an increasing number of people over 60 are taking off-peak holidays. It is sometimes reasonable to focus on the UK market (60 million people) but most small shops, for example, compete in a local market (a typical town has 100,000 people in its population). At the other end of the scale, mobile phone producers are businesses which compete in a global market with billions of potential buyers.

Tastes

Tastes and preferences also affect demand. A trend to prepared meals and eating outside the home means a growing demand for takeaway and restaurant meals. However, within this sector there has recently been a relative fall in demand for burger meals and a growth in demand for healthier foods. The target of advertising is to influence tastes, thereby increasing demand for a product or a brand.

From being a luxury item, mobile phones quite quickly became something the majority of people have. The number of handsets in the UK has overtaken the number of people over the age of 12. Increasingly, people own more than one handset. Changes in lifestyle and how fashionable products are do not necessarily stem from advertising, but to some extent our tastes are modified by advertisers when they succeed in persuading us that we want something. Advertising to influence tastes is one of the major forms of **non-price competition**.

effective demand the combination of desire for a product with ability and readiness to pay.

consumers the customers who buy and use goods and services. We are all consumers.

population structure dividing up the total population by characteristics such as age and gender.

> **Knowledge check 3**
>
> Name three businesses that sell consumer products in most countries around the world.

tastes consumer preferences for products or types of products, generally subject to shifts over time.

non-price competition seeking an advantage over rivals by using anything other than price, e.g. quality, innovation, differentiation, promotion. Successful non-price competition often leaves healthy profit margins.

Substitutes and complementary goods

substitutes alternatives to a particular product; similar brands are close substitutes.

If we are looking at one producer's output, say a particular brand, the nature and availability of alternatives will influence demand. If there are many rival brands, known in toolkit jargon as **substitutes**, demand for any one brand will be reduced and the producer will have to compete for sales. An alternative brand of the same thing is a close substitute; alternative products can also be substitutes. Bowling, for example, can be a substitute for the cinema. If other goods are used together with a product, the availability and price of these **complementary goods** is significant. Sticking with the bowling example, some people enjoy bowling more where liquid refreshment is also available.

complementary goods items that are consumed together, such as iPods and music downloads.

income money received, e.g. wages from employment.

disposable income how much people have available to spend after tax and benefits.

normal products items that we generally buy more of as income increases (e.g. clothes), unlike inferior goods.

inferior goods products we buy less of as rising income lets us switch to more attractive substitutes, e.g. bus travel.

income distribution the way that income is shared out between members of a community

price the amount paid by the buyer in a transaction to the seller.

opportunity cost the best alternative given up when we make a choice and use a resource. Examples include the next best use of a land site, of income or of time.

Incomes

In poor communities people have less **income** and buy both less and different goods and services. As **disposable incomes** rise, people have more spending power and demand more **normal products**, i.e. items such as clothes. There are exceptions (called **inferior goods**) which people move away from as they can afford better alternatives. Bus companies lost customers as rising incomes allowed more people to buy cars. Luxury products (such as holidays) are particularly likely to benefit from rising incomes. In recent decades, the most luxurious products have also gained from a less even **income distribution** in the UK, which means that more people can afford to buy a Rolex, Rolls-Royce and/or private jet. If there are more poor people as well as more rich, some inferior goods might sell well too.

Price

Price is important because paying for something means giving up alternatives (the best alternative lost when we make a choice is called the **opportunity cost**). The higher the price, the more buyers have to give up for a product, so the less they are likely to buy. Economists pay particular attention to price, using demand curves to show the link between price and quantity demanded.

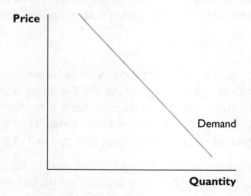

Figure 1 Demand curve

As Figure 1 shows, this 'curve' (which is often drawn as a straight line) slopes downward from left to right. This is because at a higher price a lower quantity is bought. People might switch to alternatives which now seem relatively cheaper or might choose to save their money. The convention is to show price (P) on the vertical axis and quantity (Q) on the horizontal axis. It is good practice to label 'P' and 'Q' on any diagrams in the exam.

A demand curve deals only with the link between price and quantity demanded. Therefore, if any of the other influences on demand changes, e.g. population or tastes, we have to move to a new curve. Figure 2 shows the impact of population growth (D_1) or a product going out of fashion (D_2).

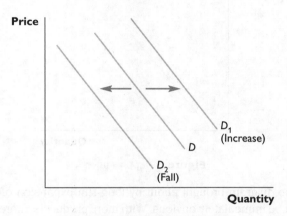

Figure 2 Changes in demand

Supply

Market supply

The combined quantity that all producers are willing to sell at any price is the **market supply**. The biggest influence on supply will be costs, as a business will want to sell if the price more than covers costs and so leaves a profit.

As a general rule, higher prices will encourage firms to supply more because extra revenue from a price increase will make it worth incurring more costs. In the **short term**, existing firms will use spare capacity and perhaps introduce overtime or other immediate ways of increasing output such as running down stocks. This is easier in some industries than others. Farmers, for example, cannot quickly produce many new crops. High prices and profits will also attract entrepreneurs to start new businesses, but this will require a longer time period before they produce and have an impact on market supply. Supply can change more in the **long run**.

The market as a signalling mechanism

One attraction of the **market system** is that profits attract entrepreneurs and act as signals to them to use resources for products people will pay most for. If demand and price fall, firms might become unprofitable and close down. This will free resources from these firms for other uses.

Each individual decision maker is motivated by their own gain, yet markets can make sound choices between alternative uses of resources. This is because people will pay

market supply the quantity that all producers of a product want to sell at a particular price.

short term a period of time in which a business cannot change fixed costs, e.g. size of premises.

long run to an economist, the long run is the time it takes to make a change in the fixed assets of a business. It is impossible to set a standard length of time here as a hairdresser (for example) might be able to install new chairs and equipment in a few weeks whereas an electricity generator would take years to construct a new plant.

market system the private enterprise system that has demand, supply, prices and profits deciding resource use, with minimal government participation.

most for things they value most, making things people value most the best sources of profit. Supply curves slope upwards from left to right to show how quantity placed on the market will rise as price does, as you can see from Figure 3.

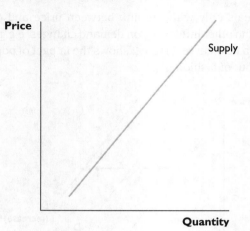

Figure 3 Supply curve

The change to the diagram brought about by long-run expansion of an industry, for example, may not be immediately obvious. With more producers, more will be supplied at any price. The supply curve will move to the right (S_1), as you can see in Figure 4. A glance at this diagram might suggest a fall in supply. This potential confusion is often tested by examiners — so be clear about this shift and equally about the leftwards shift caused by a fall in supply (perhaps due to industry shrinkage or a rise in costs).

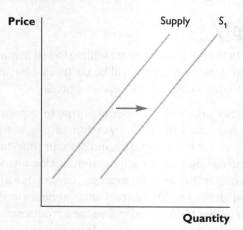

Figure 4 Increase in supply

equilibrium (point)
generally, this means being in balance. In economics and business this is most often a balance between demand and supply for a product or aggregate demand (see p. 26) and aggregate supply in an economy. Demand and supply for a product are equal at the equilibrium point where demand and supply curves intersect.

Interaction

Equilibrium point

When we put the curves together in a market diagram, we can see that with the normal slopes there will be just one intersection. This is the **equilibrium point** at which price and quantity should settle. It shows the one combination of price and quantity at which demand matches supply. As Figure 5 shows, any price above the equilibrium level (such as P_1) would entail supply exceeding demand so surplus product on the market would be unsold unless the price falls. This situation would be reversed if price was below equilibrium at P_2: demand would exceed supply and price would normally be pushed up. A shift in either curve should be followed by a move along the other curve to a new price level. You should be comfortable with showing changes on this type of diagram.

A change in any of the factors influencing demand, other than price, will cause a shift of the demand curve and a move along the supply curve to a new equilibrium price and quantity. If the supply curve shifts, that will bring a move along the demand curve to a new intersection.

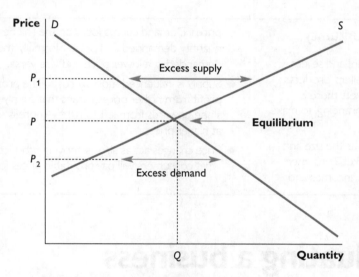

Figure 5 Demand and supply curve for Product X

When coffee bars became more fashionable, the demand curve shifted up and to the right, leading to a new higher price and quantity. Profit potential attracted new coffee bars so eventually, in this case, the supply curve shifted right too. When cheaper components reduced the cost of computers, the supply curve moved to the right and this caused a move along the demand curve to a lower price and higher quantity.

Impact of main changes in demand and supply

- **A rise in demand** shifts the demand to the right leaving a shortage at the current price, so price will rise and the equilibrium quantity will increase.
- **A fall in demand** shifts the demand curve to the left leaving a surplus at the current price, so price will fall and equilibrium quantity will fall.
- **A rise in supply** shifts the supply curve to the right leaving a surplus at the current price, so price will fall and equilibrium quantity will increase.
- **A fall in supply** shifts the supply curve to the left leaving a shortage at the current price, so price will rise and the equilibrium quantity will fall.

If you can visualise these changes, your understanding is probably sound. If not, it might help you to try drawing them. Think of recent well-publicised price changes, both up and down. Can you construct a demand and supply diagram to illustrate and explain these changes? What has caused the most recent change in oil prices, for example?

When a business is introducing a new product, the ideal demand curve is one which is nearly vertical, showing that a higher price would have little impact on how much consumers will buy. Some of the advertising for existing products is aimed at persuading customers that this is the product for them, even if its price rises. If a new brand enters a crowded market, the market supply curve will show that higher quantities are available and attracting sales will be difficult. There are clear advantages to supplying something that is new or different.

Summary

Identifying a business opportunity

- Any arrangement that allows buyers and sellers to trade is a market. Sometimes sellers' products are identical but in consumer markets there is frequently differentiation, such as branding, to make each firm's product distinctive.
- Demand depends on factors such as the size and structure of population in the market, consumer tastes, subsidies and complements, incomes and prices. Demand curves focus on the link between quantity demanded and price. Normally, more is demanded at a lower price and vice versa.
- Supply is influenced most by costs. The prospect of profit from higher prices means that supply curves slope upwards from left to right – more is supplied at higher prices.
- Price changes act as signals, moving production to what consumers will pay profitable prices for.

Evaluating a business opportunity

mass production turning out large quantities of standardised products, often using a production line and seeking economies of scale to drive down unit costs.

long tail the idea that modern markets have room for many small niche suppliers alongside larger firms that mass produce, thanks partly to technology such as the internet.

However technically advanced and well made a product is, it will not sell unless consumers prefer it to rival products. There are well-established producers and brands in many markets. This does not mean that it is necessary to challenge the market leader head on. In his book *The Long Tail: Why the Future of Business is Selling Less of More* (2006), Chris Anderson argues that changes in technology (especially the impact of computers on production and of the internet on distribution) make it possible to identify and exploit a myriad of small niche markets, producing and selling in small quantities without the cost and logistical disadvantages that might once have made such specialism unattractive. In other words, it has become easier to identify and meet the requirements of small groups with minority preferences, which are frequently ignored by large firms supplying **mass produced** standard products in large quantities. These opportunities present good potential for new firms to start up successfully and thrive by supplying '**long tail**' niches, even where there is a mass market dominated by large, strong businesses with established brands.

Researching demand

Market research

Setting up a business because you have a hunch that it might be profitable is foolish and unnecessarily risky. You might be a fan of flared trousers while others have different preferences. How many people will see things in the same way that you do, be as enthusiastic about your product and be willing to buy it at a price that meets your requirements? It is impossible to guess the answers to many such questions with any confidence. It is sensible to gather the most reliable possible information in order to inform your decision making and business planning. This information gathering process is called market research.

Think, for example, about someone contemplating setting up a nursery school. It would be useful to know how many toddlers are in the area and whether there is any new house building or a rising birth rate to suggest that there will be more toddlers in future. What do parents value most in a nursery school? What do current nursery schools charge and do they have vacancies? The ideal answers to these questions would be that they are full and have long waiting lists. Besides looking at the market, there are also complicated rules about health and safety, staffing ratios and qualifications for people working with toddlers. What are the rules? Are suitably qualified staff available, and if so at what wage level? How difficult will it be to find suitable premises and what will they cost? What equipment will be needed? All these matters, or the equivalent for other ventures, should be researched in the early stages of planning a business.

Secondary market research

Much of the necessary information can be looked up, e.g. using internet searches or reference libraries. Specialist businesses compile detailed market information, which they sell to their customers. Getting access to information that others have already gathered is called 'secondary market research', also known as 'desk research'. This can be substantially quicker and easier than collecting your own data. Most official statistics and some commercially collected data are pretty reliable, though errors can creep into even the most careful work. The company, Keynote, sells market research, and the free samples on **www.keynote.co.uk** offer information in some detail on a range of UK markets.

Primary market research

If you collect your own data, or commission others to do the job for you, this is primary market research (also called 'field research'). Quantitative market research (normally numerical) tends to generate more reliable results than qualitative market research, which deals with attitudes, preferences and feelings. A Tesco Clubcard or similar loyalty card gives the retailer significant amounts of primary quantitative market research data on shopping habits.

Sampling

There is a margin of error in market research but if the research has been done well, the results often give a reasonable indication of conditions facing a business. The

market research studying a market to gather data, particularly on factors influencing demand for the product.

Examiner tip
If you write about market research, be careful to stick to what is relevant to the business in the question.

secondary market research taking information from data already collected by others.

primary market research conducting new research into demand for a product.

quantitative market research numerical research, e.g. on potential customers or sales of rivals.

qualitative market research research into preferences and attitudes, often in some depth.

questionnaire set of questions aimed at gathering market research information, requiring careful construction to minimise bias.

sampling gathering information from a small sample rather than the whole market or population.

questionnaires and interviews on which qualitative primary research is often based need careful construction and use. Even if the questions are good, primary research about a nursery for toddlers will give biased results if most of the people questioned are pensioners (unless the area is mainly inhabited by pensioners). There are alternative approaches to **sampling**, which can improve its reliability.

One variable is the size and structure of sample used. Generally, the larger the size of samples the more reliable or 'significant' the results become. Major surveys often consult thousands of people to reach more reliable results. Samples can be 'random', where it is left to chance to get a reasonable cross section of views, with just obvious risks of bias removed. A student conducting a sampling exercise and using the most conveniently available people will generally get results biased towards the student age group. Care should be taken at least to consider the consequences of such a skewed sample. The alternative is to structure samples, with age, gender or other relevant characteristics of the people consulted kept to required proportions. However, even a structured sample can give biased results.

If you have carried out primary and secondary market research, think about the processes you followed, the difficulties you faced and how useful your results were. You should be clear about the different approaches, the value of market research and also its limitations.

Knowledge check 4

What is the basic difference between primary and secondary market research?

Task

If you have not conducted market research, the following is a sample exercise that you could plan and even carry out if you have the time available.

(1) Use secondary market research to find up-to-date information on mobile phone sales, ownership and use. (Historical data show that in 1996 mobile phones were owned by around 18% of households.)

(2) Design an unbiased questionnaire to assess the relative importance to mobile phone users of: voice calls, text messaging, camera, 3G, web access/emails, GPS, MP3 player, size/style of handset.

(3) Think through ways of obtaining results from a representative cross section of the population.

(4) If there is time, gather results and collate them.

(5) Use your results as a basis for advice to a phone maker on what a new model should include.

Is there a market?

strategy skilled direction and planning to work towards meeting long-term objectives.

tactics approaches to meeting challenges and overcoming obstacles, often specific to an immediate situation.

Identifying a potential market by using market research is only one step towards a successful business. Turning an idea with potential into a reality will require using information gained to influence both **strategy** (coordinated long-term planning) and **tactics** (approaches to individual problems). The ancient Chinese general Sun Tzu said: 'Strategy without tactics is the slowest route to victory. Tactics without strategy is the noise before defeat.' People who seem to be lucky have often worked hard and planned thoroughly. In market-orientated industries they have often worked hardest on their marketing.

Businesses have a marketing strategy designed to bring healthy sales. In Unit 2 you will learn about the **marketing mix** that coordinates aspects of marketing.

Competitive advantage

Commodity products

Few products are so standardised that customers all buy the same thing. Some '**commodity products**' come close to standardisation (e.g. milk, potatoes, petrol) but even here there is often branding and attempted differentiation. The main reason for differentiation is that firms see it as a route to a competitive advantage, which puts them ahead of rivals. Simply carrying the label of a known brand such as Nike or Chanel is a form of differentiation and can be a source of competitive advantage because of the reputation associated with such brands.

Added value

Looking at this from another perspective, a business needs to sell its products for more than the cost of its inputs (see p. 27). In toolkit terms it needs **added value**. This requires consumers to be willing to pay a high enough price because of the value they place on the product or service they are offered. A baker adds value by combining ingredients to make a desirable product. A personal trainer adds value by helping clients to feel fitter and better about their physical condition. A new business benefits from clarity on how it will add value. In many consumer markets there is a major incentive to **innovate** and introduce new products which are either technically more advanced (e.g. mobile phones, MP3 players) or more precisely meet the preferences of consumers (e.g. current music styles).

Market segments

Variations in the characteristics of products (and customers) are frequently so marked that it makes sense to subdivide a market into segments. With cars, for example, price, speed, safety, size, appearance, running costs and other features have different relative priorities to different groups of customers. One **market segment** is for large four-wheel drive 'Chelsea tractors', given this nickname because of their popularity with some affluent metropolitan families. By contrast, some quite similar families favour the 'green' segment with minimum emissions to the environment and less concern for speed or status. From a new firm's perspective, it can make sense to target a small segment or 'niche', which is relatively neglected. In the case of cars, for example, a start-up producer might be attracted to the niche for quirky sports cars, where a distinctive new model might be more attractive to a particular type of consumer, than the lower priced models offered by mass producers.

The main consumer market segmentation characteristics are:
- **age** (often by age groups, e.g. 30–45 = typically parents of young families)
- **gender** and sexual orientation
- **location** — where people live
- **social class** — linked mainly to occupation

marketing mix the blend of interdependent components used in marketing a product, often divided into product, price, place and promotion.

commodity product a standard item where there is no differentiation between the output of alternative suppliers. Minerals and basic foods have been seen as commodity products.

Examiner tip
It is easy to see how making things adds value. Services add value too, but a little more thought might be needed in order to see how.

adding value changing inputs (e.g. materials) in a way that customers see as beneficial and attractive.

value a subjective view of what something is worth.

innovation the introduction of new products, normally resulting either from technological change or from perceived market needs.

market segment a subdivision of a market with distinctive characteristics, bigger than a niche.

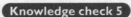

- **income**
- **behaviour** — spending patterns, brand loyalties, buying habits
- **psychological** — lifestyle, attitudes, personality, values

Building strong relationships

Another possible route to competitive advantage is to work at particularly strong relationships with stakeholders who have an interest in the business. If a business can convince customers, for example, that the business is their friend and has their interests at heart, customer loyalty is likely to result. Winning repeat business from existing customers is considered to be less expensive than attracting new customers. Many businesses claim that their workforce is their greatest asset, trying to keep staff morale high and in the process gaining the benefit of commitment and care for the work that is completed. Suppliers are another group of stakeholders; a good relationship with them can influence the reliable arrival and sometimes the quality of inputs to a product. Working at a good relationship with the local community can build a positive attitude that strengthens a business, as it can be seen both as a good employer (helping recruitment) and as 'deserving' custom and support. Sometimes there are trade-offs between the interests of different groups of stakeholders. Most obviously, added expenditure for the benefit of other stakeholder groups can reduce profits for shareholders.

Table 2 Main stakeholder groups

Stakeholder	Relationship
Shareholders	Owners of the company who generally hope for profits. A company must aim to satisfy the majority of shareholders.
Employees	Workers in a company are entitled to a safe working environment and to the agreed wage for the work they do. Training and support for workers is also normal.
Consumers	Customers of the business expect goods and services to particular qualities and standards, including legally required compliance on trade descriptions, fitness for purpose, health and safety standards.
Suppliers	Suppliers expect payment within a reasonable time period and also good communications. A poor relationship with suppliers can create major disruption.
Creditors	Anyone owed money by a business will expect payment, including banks and tax collectors for example.
Local community	People and environment of the area will feel an impact from business activity — firms have an increasing awareness of issues concerning the community and environment.

Key marketing concepts

- adding value
- commodity products
- market segments
- innovation
- reputation
- relationships

Positioning a business idea

Existing producers will be competitors for any new business, so it is important to study them and identify how they differentiate themselves (price? quality? brand?

Sidebar

Knowledge check 5

Identify three segments (not niches) in the market for clothes.

relationships in a business sense the main focus is on relationships with stakeholder groups such as customers and suppliers. Strong relationships are a source of competitive advantage.

stakeholder someone with an interest in a business and its activities, e.g. workers, suppliers, customers, local community and government.

customer loyalty when customers are likely to bring repeat business and perhaps have a sound relationship with the vendor. The conventional wisdom is that treating customers well enough to earn their loyalty is cheaper than attracting new customers.

shareholder someone who owns shares in a business and is therefore a part-owner, entitled to a share of any distributed profits.

creditor someone to whom a debt is owed, e.g. a supplier of materials or a bank that lent money.

features? reliability?). Duplicating what is already offered makes sense only if there is a serious flaw with **products** existing businesses sell. A new supplier needs to seek some competitive advantage, as explained earlier. This can sometimes be found by using segmentation analysis and/or **market mapping** to find a niche or segment which is relatively neglected by existing firms so that a newcomer can focus on it.

Market mapping

Market mapping consists of identifying key variables about a product, plotting where existing brands or suppliers are in terms of combining the variables, then identifying any gaps in the market. To take an example, some consumers prefer bland-tasting bread because it will not mask the taste of whatever they are eating with it; others like tasty bread. Some people want fibre in their bread as it is believed to be healthy; others want soft, fibre-free bread. Some years ago, fibre generally went with stronger tasting bread. In market-mapping terms, most brands would have been in the lower-left segment in the 'map' in Figure 6, near the centre or high on the right. Growing consumer concern for healthy eating led some bakers to introduce loaves with added fibre but no strong taste — mapping could have shown that this was a relatively neglected **market position**.

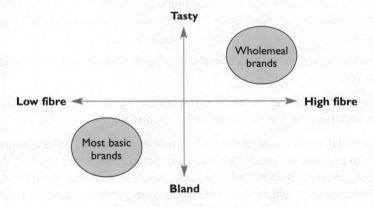

Figure 6 Market map for bread

A new entrant to a market could gain useful ideas on **product positioning** from mapping what rivals offer and seeing if there is any combination of features which is attractive to consumers yet is currently neglected.

Price

Setting a price means balancing the desire for more revenue per sale (high price) against the desire for more sales (lower price). Consumer sensitivity to price changes varies between markets. Sometimes there is intense **price competition** between firms, forcing prices down to levels offering little or no profit. In such situations, the survival of suppliers is often uncertain. Businesses frequently see the alternative of non-price competition as more attractive.

product whatever a business sells (and often also makes).

market mapping plotting the position of suppliers/brands against key characteristics of a product.

market positioning focusing a product and its marketing on a particular market segment (perhaps also considering the relative position of rivals).

product positioning choosing key characteristics in comparison to the competition, perhaps using market mapping.

price competition businesses attempting to attract sales by setting prices lower than those of rivals. Such competition is common with commodity goods but limits profit margins — many consumer goods suppliers prefer differentiation or non-price competition.

Knowledge check 6

Why might a firm reduce its price to the point where it makes no profit?

Tasks

(1) Identify two variable characteristics of a product/market that you know well. Draw up a market map and locate leading brands on it.

(2) Think of a major employer in your area. Identify stakeholder groups in this business. Are relationships with major stakeholders (a) good and (b) useful to the firm?

Product trial

Any new business needs a good idea of its product's nature and qualities before starting production. Market research and product positioning frequently cause a rethink and modifications to initial ideas. Until a product actually sells to customers, there will still be doubt about whether they are being offered precisely what they most want to buy.

product trials testing the market by selling first in a confined area to gauge demand and perhaps collecting feedback on the product and possible modifications.

cash flow a calculation or projection of cash coming into a business and payments going out. Even a profitable business can fail if it runs out of cash to pay its bills; therefore, cash flow projections are important in planning.

revenue stream the flow of revenue received over time.

Before large businesses operating nationally or globally start large-scale marketing of a new product, they will commonly conduct **product trials** in a relatively small area. UK product trials, for example, are often carried out in one ITV region for marketing convenience. Multinational companies might start with trials in a small country. Early sales can be followed up by market research on consumer reaction and on how to win repeat business. Such trialling delays a full-scale launch but has two advantages:

(1) Consumer reaction might generate information on how the product can be improved.

(2) Information on trial sales can be extrapolated to give an indication of likely total sales and therefore the required level of production.

If a product trial helps a new business to avoid expensive mistakes, to improve its product or to produce the quantities that it can actually sell in the market, then it is a valuable step to take. The downside for a new business is often in the impact on **cash flow**. Major costs will have to be incurred before any product reaches consumers and a product trial can extend the time before **revenue streams** bring necessary money into the business.

Do you think that a product trial would be worthwhile for (a) a new chocolate bar and (b) a new, local taxi/minicab business?

Opportunity cost

When any resource has limited availability, using it in one way entails giving up something else. The toolkit term 'opportunity cost' means the best alternative given up when a particular choice is made. Obvious examples are concerned with spending. If you choose to buy, say, an expensive holiday, you might have to give up ideas of changing your car. The replacement car is then the opportunity cost of taking the holiday. Money is really just a token representing ability to choose between the alternative goods and services that are available. Opportunity cost draws attention to the **trade-offs** involved in making particular decisions. Choosing each subject to study in Year 12 has the opportunity cost of whichever next best choice you reject. Time is a scarce resource too. The opportunity cost of full-time study can be just too great for some students who prioritise work and earlier income.

Exams illustrate opportunity cost too. With just 75 minutes available in this unit, spending too much time on supported multiple-choice and the simpler parts of structured data–response questions is foolish. This carries the opportunity cost that the major sections of structured data–response, which carry the biggest mark allocations, will be rushed.

Starting up a new business entails the use of a variety of resources, including time, energy and capital. It often also entails an opportunity cost of giving up paid employment and the income it generates. When someone or a group of people choose one particular business from a range of possibilities, the opportunity cost is the next best alternative business opportunity that is given up.

This emphasises the importance of making the choice that best meets your objectives, whether they are profit maximisation or something else. How interesting and how risky options are might also influence a choice. Once a choice is made, it becomes increasingly difficult to switch to an alternative.

trade-offs taking a setback in terms of one objective in order to prioritise another, e.g. having a holiday and accepting that work will suffer in the short term.

Knowledge check 7

Jot down the main differences between:

- market segments and market niches
- market orientation and market positioning
- stakeholders and shareholders
- opportunity cost and money cost

Evaluating a business opportunity

- Market research supplies valuable information for new (and existing) businesses. This can be either original (primary) research or secondary research using data already collected.
- Sampling can give a picture of the likely situation without having to survey everyone.
- Businesses seek competitive advantage, ways of getting an edge over rivals. They might specialise in providing for particular market segments. They might seek to build strong relationships with stakeholders.

- Market positioning means offering a product with features designed to appeal to some customers, perhaps customers that are neglected by rivals. Market mapping can identify neglected market positions.
- Product trials to test the market in small areas can give useful feedback and help a business to avoid expensive mistakes.
- Whatever decisions are made, there is always an opportunity cost of alternatives given up when businesses (or individuals) make a choice.

Summary

Economic considerations

Just as individuals have moods, perhaps varying from cheerful to grumpy, there are often prevailing atmospheres in groups or organisations. If we extend this to the whole community, there are variations in the 'climate' of how optimistic or pessimistic the majority of people feel. When the economic climate is optimistic people are more willing to borrow and to spend, so demand for many products is higher. When the mood is more pessimistic, people are more careful, spending less and perhaps trying to pay off some of their debts. Luxuries and large discretionary purchases, which can be postponed or abandoned, are most likely to see variations in sales. Entrepreneurs tend to be more careful about starting a business when the general mood is pessimistic.

One of the best statistical measures of the state of the economy is the growth of **gross domestic product (GDP)**. This basically measures the level of output in the economy. The long-term trend in the UK is for GDP to grow at around 2.5% per year. Faster growth means more activity and is broadly associated with a positive climate but also with a risk of inflation. Slow or even negative growth (a **recession**) tends to be associated with growing unemployment and more pessimism in business.

Although we can make reasonable generalisations, the economic climate is not set in an entirely logical and rational way. The economist J. M. Keynes referred to something called '**animal spirits**'. A major success for a national sports team can generate a feel-good factor that spills over into the economic climate. An event such as falling house prices, as seen in 2008/2009, can shake **consumer confidence**, make people more cautious and contribute to subsequent recession. Though we must allow for chance and random events, we can identify clear influences on expectations, the economic climate and behaviour.

Interest rates

Base rate

The UK 'base rate' is an **interest rate** set monthly by the **Monetary Policy Committee (MPC)** of the Bank of England. The base rate acts as an indicator around which other interest rates in the economy are set. When base rates go up, the purpose is to counter inflation. Higher interest rates mean that mortgage interest payments go up for many house buyers. Some mortgage interest payments are closely tied to base rates, others are fixed for a period of time and so only rise after a time lag. Increased mortgage payments take up more income and leave less to spend on everything else, so demand for some products will fall.

In addition, rising interest rates are taken as a sign that economic conditions will grow more difficult, making people less optimistic. Large purchases, which tend to be funded by borrowing, are vulnerable to postponement or cancellation when interest rates rise. This is true for consumers and for businesses. Many businesses have loans or **overdrafts**, so rising interest rates will increase their costs.

The extent to which costs will increase depends on how much interest rates rise and on how much the business has borrowed. The overall effect of higher interest rates will be to reduce total demand in the economy (known as **aggregate demand** or **AD**), so life will get harder for the average business.

There are people and businesses who will not feel adverse effects. People who save are likely to see the interest paid on their savings increase and firms with no debt will not have a cost increase directly resulting from higher interest rates. Despite this, most businesses are likely to prefer the reverse situation in which cuts in interest rates stimulate spending and activity, while also making many people feel better off. The MPC will cut interest rates when the risk of inflation seems less than

---

gross domestic product (GDP) the main measure of economic activity and output in the UK.

recession a period of falling output and rising unemployment; technically two or more successive quarters of falling GDP.

animal spirits J. M. Keynes's name for swings between optimism and pessimism in the community, which are often not rational.

consumer confidence how optimistic consumers are, which influences their attitude to spending.

interest rate the charge paid by borrowers to lenders for loans.

Monetary Policy Committee (MPC) the team (of nine) assembled by the Bank of England to take monthly decisions on the base rate, which heavily influences other interest rates in the UK.

overdraft an agreement with a bank that you can borrow an amount up to a set limit for a period of time.

aggregate demand (AD) a measure of all the spending in the economy by consumers, firms, government and overseas buyers of exports.

Examiner tip
Base rate changes tend to be small. Beware of exaggerating the effects of one small change.

the risk of demand and activity falling. This is commonly done when there are signs of recession. Deliberate use of interest rates to influence the level of activity is known as **monetary policy**.

Inflation

Inflation measures the rise in the general level of prices, generally over a 1-year period. **Hyperinflation** is extreme inflation that damages people's faith in money and hampers economic activity. For Zimbabwe in early 2008 it was hard to get a precise measure of inflation, partly because there were so few goods in the shops, but estimates suggested an annual rate of many thousand per cent. Its economy had and still has serious problems that some people feel will lead to meltdown or collapse. In the UK in the 1970s, inflation at over 20% per annum had an unsettling effect on the economic climate.

With rapid inflation, many businesses are uncertain about how costs will change and their ability to pass on rising costs of their **inputs** to customers. There are also extra costs associated with frequently changing price lists and with shopping around as supplier prices change. Consumers are uncertain about what they can afford and whether their income will keep pace with prices. This is likely to make them more cautious and perhaps reduce their spending. One feature working in the opposite direction is that house price inflation can make people feel that they have become wealthier because their house is worth more, if they are owner occupiers or mortgage payers. A '**wealth effect**' can lead people to spend more. This is an illustration of why there is confusion and uncertainty at times of inflation.

For its first 10 years (to 2007) the Monetary Policy Committee seemed very successful at keeping inflation close to its target. More recently, global increases in fuel and food prices have contributed to higher inflation levels.

Consumer price index (CPI)

The current UK inflation target is 2% per annum, measured by the **consumer price index** (CPI). When countries experience negative inflation (falling prices), this indicates low levels of demand and a pessimistic economic climate. Low single figure inflation seems consistent with an economic climate in which many businesses are comfortable. The MPC is responsible for changing interest rates to stay within 1% of the inflation target.

The CPI is directly used for purposes such as adjusting pensions and other benefits to compensate for the effects of inflation. Less directly, it is also a factor influencing price setting and wage negotiations.

Unemployment

The level of **unemployment** is another important variable. At times and in places with high unemployment, people are less secure about future incomes and therefore more reluctant to spend. A recession is a period of falling income and employment.

Knowledge check 8

How might a cut in interest rates stimulate spending and activity?

monetary policy use of the Bank of England base rate to influence economic and business activity, targeting 2% inflation measured by the consumer price index.

inflation a sustained rise in the general level of prices, normally measured over a year, either by the consumer price index or the retail price index.

hyperinflation situation in which prices rise so rapidly that people lose confidence in money, typically with hundreds or thousands of percentage price rises per year.

inputs things such as material and labour that go into the production process. Inputs are normally costs to a business.

wealth effect feeling better off (wealthier) because the value of assets (e.g. your house) has risen.

consumer price index (CPI) a measure of the rate of inflation, based on a weighted collection of prices to represent typical consumer spending.

unemployment being willing to work and available for work but not having a job.

redundancies making
unwanted workers in a
firm unemployed, often
because demand is too low
or technology has changed.

Knowledge check 9

Why are full-time
students not counted as
unemployed?

full employment a
situation where most
people who want paid
employment have a job.
Some unemployment is
inevitable and included in
full employment.

income tax the biggest
revenue-raising tax paid
by UK individuals, based
on their earnings and any
other income.

value added tax (VAT)
the main UK tax on
expenditure, currently 20%
added to the price of most
products.

benefits gains,
often payments from
government, for example to
pensioners, households with
children or the disabled.

public spending
government and local
authority spending on
goods, services and
benefits paid to members
of the community.

Lower incomes leave people less money to spend, and the fear of unemployment can further cut spending. If consumers buy less, firms will tend to produce less and this can lead to **redundancies** and increased unemployment. Starting a business in this type of situation is extra risky because of uncertain demand. Low unemployment is associated with a more optimistic economic climate.

Regional variations within the UK (and many other countries) have long been a feature of unemployment. Broadly speaking, London and the southeast have the biggest concentration of customers and are long established as the main base for many service industries such as banking and finance. Unemployment rates have tended to be higher away from the southeast, often increasing as distance from London increases. For example, the North of Scotland (until North Sea Oil), Northern Ireland and Cornwall have had relatively high rates of unemployment for decades.

From the perspective of businesses employing people, relatively high unemployment makes it easier to recruit workers. Areas with high unemployment often have some other lower costs too, with less competition for premises, for example. With low unemployment (also called '**full employment**') finding people can be harder and retaining existing staff can become an issue. Unemployment is healthy for recruiting but this factor conflicts with a preference for full employment when selling most products to consumers.

Because unemployment is often localised, it is sometimes possible for a business to expand its production activities in an area of high unemployment and sell its products in other areas where economic conditions and demand are more attractive. Multinational companies can extend this approach globally by concentrating manufacturing activities in China and other Asian countries, for example.

Taxation

Tax increases reduce disposable income (the amount people can actually spend) and make people feel poorer, even before the impact of the proposed tax increase reaches them. This is most obvious with **income tax**, which is the government's biggest individual source of income. Businesses collect **value added tax** (**VAT**) for the government, mainly by adding the tax to prices, and also pay corporation tax on their profits and tax on employing people. Like consumers, businesses are cheered by tax cuts that reduce the amount they have to pay. In recent years, lower tax for firms has been aimed partly at attracting business to the country.

At the same time as preferring lower taxes, people expect to receive services provided by national and local government. Governments also pay social security **benefits** (e.g. pensions) to individuals and give some grants and services to businesses. Like tax cuts, extra **public spending** (spending by the government) increases the amount of money in the economy and so can boost the economic climate and activity.

Many individuals dislike completing tax returns. Businesses need to keep careful records and file detailed returns, giving them significant costs even before they hand over their own tax payments and any tax they have collected from others. Every time that taxes are reformed this creates extra chores for business. When businesses fail, the creditors most impatient for overdue payments will often include the tax authorities.

Governments deliberately use a deficit (when spending exceeds income) or a surplus (more taxation than spending) to influence the economy and business activity. This process is known as **fiscal policy**. A surplus entails taking more out of the **private sector** in tax than the government is putting back in by spending. This will reduce activity (and inflationary pressure) unless there are other conflicting changes going on. A **public sector** deficit will add to private sector incomes, so is expected to stimulate more spending and activity. Such a deficit is financed by borrowing. Countries such as Greece, Ireland and Portugal have shown in recent years that a big build-up of government borrowing can damage confidence in a country.

Exchange rates

If businesses source products or component materials from abroad, or if they sell to overseas customers, they are influenced by the **exchange rates** between the pound sterling and other currencies. In late 2007, £1 exchanged for $2. If, say, a computer assembler wanted US components priced at $15,000, the cost in pounds would be £7,500. In mid 2010 £1 exchanged for roughly $1.50 so the $15,000 dollars worth of components would have cost £10,000. Thus, a **strong pound** (more of other currencies for each pound) reduces costs for **importers**. By contrast, an American thinking of taking a holiday in the UK in 2008 would have needed to find $200 per night to pay for a £100 hotel room; a strong pound makes UK products expensive for foreigners. At £1 = $1.50 in 2010 the same priced room would have cost an American $150 per night. Any British **exporters** who compete with producers in other countries are put at a disadvantage by a strong pound. Exporters are more comfortable when the pound is weaker.

The UK's biggest trading partners in recent years have been the European Union countries, which use the **euro**, so fluctuations of the pound against the euro have a large impact. In late 2007 both the pound and the euro were strong against the $US. The European Airbus Consortium is struggling to sell passenger planes as its main rival, Boeing, is from the USA. The weak dollar makes Boeing planes cheaper in other currencies; this makes Airbus less price competitive and has led to some of its European aircraft workers being made redundant. The fall in the value of the pound against the euro in 2008 has helped British exporters but made mainland European goods more expensive in the UK.

When the pound loses value this makes imports dearer and can add to inflationary pressure, which, in turn, might prompt an increase in interest rates. When President George Bush said: 'More and more of our imports are from overseas', his intention was probably to say that more and more of US consumer goods are imported. This is true for the UK too. A consequence of this is that import prices and exchange rates have an ever greater impact on the UK economy. This has been a contributor to recent UK inflation. When there are major currency fluctuations with values moving up and down, this creates uncertainty which is unsettling for business and the economy.

fiscal policy use of a balance, or more often imbalance, between taxation and public spending to influence output, employment and inflation levels.

private sector all the parts of the economy owned by individuals and groups of people (including companies), rather than by government or other 'public sector' bodies.

public sector organisations and activities owned and controlled by the state (or local authorities) rather than by private individuals or groups.

exchange rate the price paid for one currency in terms of another, for example £1 = $2.

strong pound a high value of the pound sterling against other currencies, making imports cheap and exports dear.

imports goods or services made overseas that importers bring into the country or which UK citizens use overseas, for which payment leaves the country. Examples might be Audi cars and Spanish hotel rooms.

exports goods and services sold to overseas customers, which bring payments into the country. Rolls-Royce aircraft engines and BA revenue from overseas are examples.

Check your grasp of policy options by deciding which way each of the following could be changed to encourage lower unemployment:

- income tax
- government spending
- interest rates
- exchange rate of the pound

Tasks

(1) Check the current values of:
- the bank base rate
- pound sterling against the US dollar and the euro
- UK level of unemployment
- latest UK growth data

(2) Can you find evidence to suggest whether the prevailing economic climate is currently optimistic or pessimistic? Do the values you checked have any link to the current economic climate?

Summary

Economic considerations

- The state of the economy can create problems and opportunities for firms.
- Key measures of the economy are GDP (Gross Domestic Product), measuring total output, and AD (Aggregate Demand), which measures all the demand in the economy.
- Changes in GDP are closely linked to business confidence, an important influence on decisions. Interest rates are a cost when borrowing (as many businesses do). They also influence consumer behaviour; high interest rates discourage household borrowing and spending.
- Inflation, which is mainly measured by the Consumer Price Index (CPI), brings uncertainty at more than moderate levels. Both high inflation and negative inflation (falling prices) create difficulties for business and have an unsettling effect.

- Unemployment means wanting to work and being available but having no job. High unemployment makes it easier for firms to recruit, but also means that some consumers have little income and others might spend carefully if afraid of unemployment.
- Governments tax both businesses and individuals. They also provide some services and financial benefits. Fiscal policy involves a deliberate imbalance between government spending and receipts in order to influence AD and GDP.
- Exchange rates are the prices a currency is worth in terms of other currencies. When a currency is strong (= buys more foreign currency), imports of both resources for business and products for consumers are cheaper. When a currency is weak, imports are dearer but exports are more competitive.

Financing the new business idea

Why borrow?

Even those businesses that do not prioritise profit will need money, both to get started and to meet operating costs. Only people from rich families and lottery winners can avoid the need to balance their books. Few new businesses are cheap to set up in developed economies. There is a contrast here with developing economies where micro-credit schemes offering small loans to start-up businesses can often kick-start faster economic development. In the UK, the **start-up costs** of a mobile hairdresser or a window cleaner working alone will be relatively limited, but most businesses require premises, machinery, materials and other inputs.

Once businesses start operating, there is likely to be a **time lag** between production and the arrival of any revenue. If the customers are other businesses, for example, it is normal to leave a number of weeks between receipt of goods and payment for them (see 'Cash flow' on p. 37). This will increase the funding necessary before the business has a stream of revenue. Potentially profitable businesses often fail because of cash flow difficulties.

Many people start a business at least partly in order to make money. They are commonly surprised when they calculate how much capital they will need to find in order to get the business operating. Only a minority of new entrepreneurs will have adequate funding of their own readily available. Some might have assets that can be used. Once a homebuyer has been paying a mortgage for a few years, the general upward trend in house prices makes it probable that they will have a substantial share in the ownership of the property (known as **equity**). It is possible to get access to some of this equity by remortgaging or taking a second mortgage. This is one source of finance for a business. Future mortgage payments will be higher but, if the business succeeds, profits can cover this. If the business fails, there is a risk of losing your house and being left with nothing.

Governments like to encourage enterprise because new firms create jobs, can increase competition in the economy and can contribute to economic growth. From time to time there have been grants, loans and other incentives, such as the Enterprise Allowance Scheme, aimed at encouraging new business start-ups. Some local authorities have subsidised workshops, for example, to encourage business start-ups in their areas. Regional Development Agencies work to attract and support job creation in parts of the country with relatively high unemployment. Special tax allowances and simplifications are sometimes offered as another incentive to new businesses. Even when official help is limited to advice services rather than cash, it is worthwhile checking to see what official help is available.

Many new businesses have to borrow. Lenders like to see that the entrepreneur has put some money of his or her own into the business, even if it is only a small part of what is needed. The most accessible people to borrow from are often members of the family and friends. There are three important questions here. First, do family and friends have the necessary amounts of money available? Second, are they willing to put their money into a business where there must be a degree of risk? How will the borrower and the lender(s) feel if the business fails? It would be wrong to expect failure but it is necessary to accept that this is a possibility.

An advantage of private loans is that the terms are often relatively generous, with limited interest charged and flexible/long repayment time periods. A disadvantage is that a relative or friend who has lent money to the business will feel entitled to make their views known, sometimes in ways which might seem to amount to interference. This can lead to strained relationships unless there is a clear understanding on how far they will be kept informed, consulted and allowed to influence business decisions.

start-up costs the expenditure in setting up a new business that allows it to function.

time lags gaps often found between cause and effect, e.g. between a change in output and a change in revenue.

Knowledge check 11

What is the essential difference between profit and cash flow?

equity in general speech, fairness. In finance, equity means ownership of assets such as houses or shares. In the specific context of company accounts, equity is the name for shareholders' funds.

Examiner tip

Governments and local authorities try to help new businesses as they create jobs and incomes, but they also tax and regulate business. Many businesses see authorities as more of a problem than a help.

bank loan a fixed amount borrowed from a bank, normally with set repayments of the loan plus interest over a fixed time period.

> **Examiner tip**
> Remember that banks rarely make long-term business loans. They might renew loans or overdrafts to firms, but this cannot be taken for granted.

business plan document setting out a proposal for a new business, important for planning and for raising capital.

collateral something of value used to guarantee repayment of a loan, e.g. a house.

lease a rental agreement for use of productive assets (such as shops and machinery) for a set time.

trade credit willingness of suppliers to delay payment from their business customers for goods or services supplied.

sole trader an individual who owns and controls a business (but might have employees and not work alone).

partnership a business structure where 2–20 people share legal ownership and control. Partnership is common in professions such as law and medicine.

partnership agreement document setting out details of control, ownership and profit sharing between partners.

Bank loans and overdrafts

The next obvious option for getting a loan is a high street bank. These banks make some of their profit by using customers' deposits to finance loans and overdrafts for other customers. A **bank loan** is for a fixed amount with repayments over a fixed period. An overdraft has the advantage that the borrower can choose how much money to take, up to a set limit, and only pays interest on the amount used. Borrowing from banks, however, has two major limitations:

(1) Banks are reluctant to commit to lending for a long time period; a mortgage might run for 25 years whereas a bank loan is more often limited to around 3 years. This means that the business will need to generate revenue to repay a bank loan fairly quickly.

(2) Banks are reluctant to lend unless they are confident that they will get back any loan they make plus the interest due on it. For a business start-up loan they will generally want to see a **business plan** and will need to be persuaded that the business has a good chance of succeeding. They are more likely to lend if the borrower has assets that can be reclaimed if payments are not made (called **collateral**) and if they can see that the borrower has committed his or her own resources to the business.

Other financing options

Another possibility for small businesses is that they can **lease** premises and equipment rather than buy them outright, so avoiding large initial payments. Shops are commonly leased (rented for a fixed period of years), as are motor vehicles and specialist equipment used by many businesses. Suppliers of materials, who stand to gain from the custom of the business, will often advance generous **trade credit**, delaying payment for their supplies. This, too, can reduce the amount of start-up funding required. Businesses are often financed from a mixture of sources. New businesses, in particular, might need every source of funding they can get.

Partnerships

Up to this point, this section has been based largely on the situation of a single proprietor, or **sole trader**, setting up a new small business. Other forms of ownership can be linked to additional funding possibilities. Even if a loan comes from a family member, the lender could become a **partner** who shares the ownership of the business. Some partners contribute their efforts while others might just put money into a business. Such arrangements are normally formalised in a **partnership agreement**.

Bigger businesses

An established business, even if small, will have a track record that will reduce the amount of risk in lending to it. A small business that wishes to expand might also be generating enough profit to fund expansion internally. Many successful small businesses, which could potentially pay out substantial profits to their owners, choose instead to retain profit within the business to finance future growth. Funding growth from profit brings less risk and avoids interest payments, but might be slow. This also has an opportunity cost to the owner of not getting access to the profits for personal use, at least until growth brings higher future profit.

For a medium to large business, there are venture capitalists and specialist financial institutions that will either make loans or put money into the business for a share of its ownership. When Craig Sams, who started Green & Black's Chocolate, wanted to expand, he chose this route. A second expansion was funded when Cadbury Schweppes took over the business. It is not normal for a small start-up business to obtain funding in this way. More often, this approach helps a small established business to expand or managers to 'buy out' an existing business and become its owners. However, 'Dragons' Den' shows that venture capitalists do sometimes get involved in start-up businesses.

Private and public companies

Setting up a company opens up the possibility of raising money by issuing shares. Private limited companies have a maximum of 50 shareholders, cannot advertise shares publicly and their shareholders are often family, friends or workmates. Private companies can be small and are often set up for tax advantages and limited liability (see below) rather than to raise money. A public company (PLC) has the advantage that it can advertise shares to the public but the disadvantage of greater regulation and bureaucracy (e.g. over issuing 'articles', a 'prospectus' and being required to have an annual general meeting for shareholders). Ordinary shares give the shareholders part ownership of the company and entitle them to share in any profits. The costs associated with public companies effectively restrict them to large businesses. When Eurotunnel started, for example, it wanted to raise £5 billion for construction so set up a PLC.

Both private and public companies gain from limited liability, which means that a company gets a legal identity that is separate from that of its owners so, if it goes into debt, it is only the company's assets that can be lost. A sole trader can lose everything he or she owns if the business accumulates enough debt. If you started a business with your uncle as a partner (who supplied funds) and it failed, both your assets and his could be taken to settle business debts. To avoid this, and sometimes also because of possible tax benefits, even small businesses often become (private) companies.

Task

List strengths and weaknesses of the following ways of raising start-up capital for a small business, and decide which one you would want to use if you were starting your own business:
- loan from relatives
- bank loan
- venture capital
- partnership (with a wealthy partner)

venture capitalists specialists in lending money to new or expanding businesses, in return for either interest or part-ownership.

shares a legal claim on part-ownership of a business.

private limited company a business that has limited liability and at least one shareholder, but cannot offer shares for public sale. Many small businesses become private limited companies for tax advantages or the safety of limited liability.

public (limited) company a company that has limited liability and can advertise and sell shares to the public.

limited liability a safeguard given to shareholders. If a business fails, its shareholders/owners are not liable for its debts beyond any amount they still owe for their shares. Without this, owning shares would involve far more risk.

Summary

Financing the new business idea

- There is a time lag between starting a business and becoming profitable. Even reaching future profitability cannot normally be completely guaranteed. Start-up and other costs will occur before revenue can grow.
- Entrepreneurs are rarely capable of entirely financing their own business.
- Private loans from relatives and friends can be one source of finance. These could be comparatively inexpensive but could come with strings attached.
- Banks provide loans (fixed amounts) and overdrafts (variable up to a limit) for short to medium time periods. They are likely to lend only when the risk of losing their money is very low.
- Venture capitalists specialise in putting money into expanding businesses in return for part-ownership.
- Companies can raise money by issuing shares. Public limited companies (PLCs) can advertise shares to members of the public. New businesses are very rarely able to become PLCs straight away.

Measuring the potential success of a business idea

Estimating sales, costs and profit

As explained on pp. 19–20, sensible new businesses will use market research as a basis for estimating **sales volume**, the amount of their product that they will be able to sell. One of the key decisions to be made is on price. There are fundamentally three approaches to this decision, though it is possible to combine elements of more than one of these:

(1) **Cost-plus pricing** — this entails estimating likely costs and adding a profit margin.

(2) Looking at the prices charged by competitors (perhaps a **price leader**) and setting a price in relation to theirs. Many new businesses start by pitching their prices below those of rivals in an effort to attract custom and build market share. As they become known and sales increase, they hope to be able to raise prices to more profitable levels.

(3) **Demand-based pricing** — this depends on estimating what customers will be willing to pay.

Whichever of these approaches is used, a price that at least covers the costs of the business is generally necessary for survival.

Variable costs

Costs are normally divided into two types. Those costs which change whenever output changes are known as **variable costs** or **direct costs**. Most physical products are made from raw materials and/or components and it is obvious that, in order to produce more, it will be necessary to use more materials. Thus materials

sales volume the physical quantity of product sold in a time period.

cost-plus pricing setting prices by calculating the level of costs and then adding a margin for profit. The size of this margin varies.

price leader a business followed by competitors when it makes price changes.

demand-based pricing setting prices in accordance with how much consumers are willing to pay.

variable costs those costs, such as raw materials, that change with the level of output even in the short term. (Variable and direct costs are effectively identical.)

direct costs expenses arising immediately from production, such as materials. The direct cost of each unit is simpler to calculate than the indirect costs associated with it.

and components are a variable cost. Even service providers, such as taxi drivers and hairdressers, will use variable amounts of inputs such as fuel and shampoo.

Fixed costs

Costs that do not change for a period of time (even when output varies) are called fixed costs, overheads or indirect costs. Rent for premises and lease payments for machinery are obvious examples. These costs are not necessarily fixed forever — in time a business could move to bigger or smaller premises, for example — but they do not change with the quantity produced in the immediate way that variable costs do.

Wages and salaries need to be treated carefully when separating variable and fixed costs. Some employees have contracts with fixed wages or salaries so payments to them are a fixed cost. When people are paid by the hour worked or by the amount produced (called piece rates), or on overtime, this is a variable cost — at least in part.

If a business considers only its variable costs when setting price, there is risk of bankruptcy. At the same time, separating out the two types of costs can help in price setting and in analysing why a business has made a particular profit or loss.

Breakeven analysis

At any price, there will be a quantity of sales that is just enough to balance the books and above which the business will become profitable. Breakeven analysis identifies this quantity. As long as the price set is above variable costs, each sale will make a contribution towards fixed costs or profit. If, for example, a music CD sells to retailers at £5.50 and the variable cost of production is just 50p, the contribution is £5. This is obviously not all profit because making a recording and acquiring the machinery to produce CDs are just two examples of the fixed costs that must be met. If the fixed costs are £10,000 and the contribution is £5, sales of 2,000 CDs are necessary to break even. At this point, fixed costs (£10,000) plus variable costs (2,000 × £0.50) will just be covered by revenue (2,000 × £5.50 = £11,000). Once sales rise above 2,000 CDs, revenue will be greater than costs and so there will be profit.

Take another example. Two friends might decide, as a first business venture, to operate a baked potato stall at a 3-day music festival. The fully equipped stall is available at £400 per day, which might seem expensive but there will be thousands of people at the festival who will want to eat. Prepared potatoes plus toppings can be bought in at £0.75 each and the expected selling price is £1.75. This means that the contribution (price received minus variable costs) will be £1 per potato. With £400 fixed costs it will be necessary to sell 400 potatoes per day to break even.

The value of breakeven analysis is that the friends could now consider how likely they are to reach sales of 400 potatoes per day. If they want a margin of safety to allow for unanticipated costs or minor problems, or to target a certain profit each day, they will need to sell still more. This sounds like a lot of potatoes, maybe 500. Can the stall and the friends cope with this quantity? Will festival-goers want to buy this

fixed costs business costs, such as rent, which do not vary in the short run but can be changed in the long run.

overheads indirect costs that are not tied to specific products. Rent and administration costs are examples.

indirect costs costs not linked to specific output and not changing with short-run output changes. Such costs are also called fixed costs or overheads.

piece rates payment systems based on quantity of output rather than (for example) hours worked.

Knowledge check 12
Distinguish clearly between variable and fixed costs.

breakeven (point) the level of output at which fixed and variable costs are just covered. Sales beyond this level bring profit.

contribution what is left after direct costs have been subtracted from the revenue gained from a sale. It can be used to meet fixed costs, or be part of profit once fixed costs have been covered.

Examiner tip
Note that the breakeven point is a physical quantity of output (potatoes in this example) rather than an amount of money.

margin of safety a small surplus of planned revenue over planned costs to allow for unforeseen developments.

many? What if the price is increased? This depends partly on how much **competition** there is. The weather will play a part too, but exactly how is unclear. Poor weather might keep people away or could make them want more hot food. One function of breakeven analysis is to generate important questions for market research. If you get a breakeven exam question, it is best to be explicit about assumptions you make and to identify extra information that would be helpful.

Profit

competition a situation where rivals battle for desired outcomes: for example, rival businesses compete for market share and sales. Such competition is thought to protect the interests of consumers and to promote efficiency.

sales revenue total income received from sales of a product in a time period.

turnover the total revenue received by a business in a time period.

gross profit sales revenue minus direct (or variable) costs, ignoring other costs. This can be an amount or a percentage of sales revenue (known as gross profit margin).

cost of sales the direct cost of things used in the productive process, such as labour and materials. It excludes all overheads.

operating profit gross profit minus overheads, one of the key figures on company profit and loss accounts.

operating profit margin operating profit (as above) as a percentage of turnover.

Profitability depends upon **sales revenue** (also called **turnover** or sometimes total revenue) being greater than costs. A profit-maximising business wants the surplus of revenue over costs to be as great as possible. Because we look at different costs in different ways, we also have more than one measure of profit. **Gross profit** is revenue minus variable costs (which are sometimes called **cost of sales**). It is easy to get confused with the terminology here, with more than one name for the same thing. Turnover minus cost of sales, or revenue minus variable costs, can be used as measures of gross profit.

> gross profit = sales revenue – variable costs

Because fixed costs (= overheads) have been ignored, gross profit is not a good measure of the overall profitability of a business. It does at least tell us whether activities have created a contribution towards fixed costs or profit. Public limited companies must file annual accounts and these are relatively easy to access, especially with internet access. If you compare the accounts of a few businesses, you will see that some do not calculate gross profit at all. For those that do, there are differences in which costs are counted as fixed or variable. A simple gross profit figure or margin (gross profit as a percentage of turnover) means relatively little without additional information.

A more significant measure of profitability is **operating profit**, which is sales revenue minus both variable and fixed costs. As with gross profit, this can be expressed either as a money total or as a percentage of sales revenue. The percentage figure is known as the **operating profit margin**. Variations in business strategies entail different approaches to profit margins. The large supermarket chains sell at competitive prices that keep operating profit margins low, often around 5%, but sell such large quantities that total money operating profit can be healthy.

For example, 5% of say £20 billion gives a total profit of £1 billion. If a small antiques shop, say with a turnover of £1,000 per week, had a 5% operating profit margin, its profit would be £50 per week or £2,600 per year. The shop needs a strategy with a bigger operating profit margin, unless the costs already include a healthy 'wage' for the owner.

> operating profit = sales revenue – (variable + fixed) costs.

$$\text{operating profit margin} = \frac{\text{operating profit} \times 100}{\text{sales revenue}}$$

When a profit level is unsatisfactory or even negative, the business must look at increasing revenue, reducing costs, or both. Can prices be increased without losing custom? Can the product be improved, with extra added value, so that revenue will rise more than costs? Can either fixed or variable costs be cut without leading to a fall in revenue? Monitoring of profit levels, ratios and trends can give a warning of problems before a crisis occurs.

Cash flow

Projections of costs, revenues and profits for new businesses can be misleading if they ignore cash flow. This predicts or records the flow of money into a business in any time period (its revenue) and payments taking money out of the business (its costs). Most businesses will incur significant start-up costs before any revenue is received. Retail businesses have the advantage that customers generally pay up instantly when they make a purchase, even if it can take a short time to process payments made using credit cards. If stocks are bought in using trade credit (delayed payment), it is likely that some revenue will be received before the corresponding payment to suppliers is made.

The situation changes when small businesses are supplying goods or services to larger firms. In this situation it is normal to use **invoices** (bills) requesting payment in 28 days. Unfortunately, it is also common for small firms to be kept waiting for payments due from larger firms, often for 2 months or more. If you have the opportunity, ask the proprietor of a small business about his/her experience of this. Even a potentially profitable business can fail if it runs out of cash because receipts are delayed and payments are overdue. This makes it important to plan cash flow projections, to ensure that sufficient money is available for payments to be made and to monitor the situation with invoices awaiting settlement.

Task

Find sets of accounts for two large businesses (either from your teacher's resources or online). Find or calculate their operating profit margins. How reliable are these figures as a guide to the success of the businesses?

Examiner tip

Questions often require comments on gross or operating profit data. Comparing the figures with other years or other firms can be a good basis for comments if you have this kind of information available.

invoices bills issued for goods and services wherever immediate cash payment is not normal, generally setting out amounts due and expected payment terms.

Knowledge check 13

Why is it important for a firm to stay aware of its cash flow position?

Measuring the potential success of a business idea

- Some idea of likely sales volume is needed to decide how much to produce. Pricing is important here. Three main approaches to pricing are cost-plus, demand based and following a price leader.

- Variable or direct costs are those that change straightaway with the level of output. Fixed costs (or overheads) cannot change as quickly; this involves, for example, extra machines or bigger premises.

- Breakeven is the level of output at which total revenue catches up with total costs. Obviously,

businesses want at least this level of sales and preferably to have a margin of safety beyond breakeven.

- Turnover or sales revenue is the money coming into a business. We have two measures of profit: gross profit measures revenue minus variable costs and the more useful operating profit measures revenue minus all costs.

- Cash flow depends on the inflow of receipts and outflow of payments. Even a potentially profitable business has problems if too many payments are due before money comes in.

Summary

Putting a business idea into practice

Why plan?

Attitudes to planning vary enormously. Some people are reluctant to set off for an evening out before planning when to be where and how to proceed. Others either prefer uncertainty, letting events unfold in their own way, or perhaps they simply can't be bothered to plan and prepare. The more complicated and significant the events and developments that are involved, the more valuable planning becomes. Most weddings are carefully planned, for example. Careful preparation and planning before important interviews is sensible. Some people seem to let their lives drift on without thinking much about what is happening to them and why. Others have clear targets and ambitions, which they pursue in a highly organised way.

Getting a business operating takes detailed strategy, planning and preparation to move from ideas to reality. Making a business plan might be less fun than dreaming about success, but has important functions. In building a word picture of a business proposal, the planner is forced to identify and address areas of fuzzy thinking. A business plan raises questions that show where further research is needed. Vitally, it provides evidence for a bank or other lender that the proposal has been thought through and (hopefully) has a good chance of generating profit in order to repay loans.

Many banks issue advice pamphlets for drawing up business plans and give samples of their preferred layout. There are companies that specialise in making business plans for would-be entrepreneurs, and computer software programs are available to help people to draw up their own plan. A web search using 'business plan' as key words will come up with a variety of resources.

> **Knowledge check 14**
>
> Why do banks and other lenders like to see a business plan for start-up businesses?

What is included?

The subheadings in a business plan are not standardised, so variation is possible, but there are areas that every plan should cover. These include:
- business name, type and aims
- product and proposed price
- market information (often from research)
- personnel
- suppliers and likely production costs
- premises and equipment
- profit and cash flow estimates
- financing arrangements

How accurate?

Some factual information such as the business name should be completely accurate. **Financial information** on pricing, revenue, costs and profit will be best estimates, hopefully based on careful research, but is unlikely to be completely accurate. Potential lenders will scrutinise financial estimates. If the business is only using its plan to raise finance, there might be little interest in the plan once money has been raised. A more sensible approach is to use the plan as a template to be amended by real data once this becomes available. This will give a continuing picture of progress made, the prospects of success and whether intended actions need to be amended.

financial information data on costs, revenues and profits, a key part of a business plan.

Sample business plan

Bradford Bakers' Café

The business

Bradford Bakers' Café is a start-up business and is a partnership between David James and Sue Field. David has a background in accounting and has recently completed an in-store baking course. Sue has a retail background including 8 years as manager of a large store, which included a café. The café will sell baked goods and a variety of hot and cold drinks, in the town of Bradford-on-Avon. An option has been secured to lease a Georgian building that has already been converted for retail use, in the centre of this small tourist town. Local competition has been reduced by the retirement of a café proprietor whose premises are to be taken over by an antiques shop. None of the large coffee shop chains has a branch in the town.

Production

The leased coffee and espresso machine will enable the café to offer a wide range of coffee-based drinks of high quality, to drink in the café or to take away. Offering a broad range of teas is relatively simple. A high-class supplier of part baked and frozen bread, pastries and savoury goods has been advising the proprietors. The foundations for a good working relationship have been laid. Baking in small batches through the day is expected to maintain a supply of hot cakes, pastries and fresh bread. An attractive suggested layout for the premises is in Appendix 1. Although the aroma of fresh bread and coffee will be continuing assets, the proprietors will respond to the market by adding other lines to meet demand.

The market

Retail coffee sales in the UK have experienced rapid growth in recent years. There is a discernible shift in bakery products from the low price and mass produced to higher quality at higher prices. This trend is most marked in relatively high income areas such as Bradford-on-Avon (see Appendix 2). Middle to higher income locals are an important target market for the business, and are expected to generate 60% of revenue. Bradford-on-Avon is a picturesque small town that attracts significant

numbers of tourists. The well-located Georgian premises will help to attract tourist business. Existing rivals frequently have queues of customers in summer, even without in-store bakery facilities.

Human resources

Knowledge check 15

Will labour be a fixed cost or a variable cost for this business?

The two partners and two employees (one a baker) will work full time. There is a plentiful supply of part-time and seasonal workers in the area, particularly mothers returning to work and students. The initial intention is to use four part-timers throughout the year plus seasonal staff in summer. This planning is flexible.

Costs, revenues, profit and cash flow

A total of £100,000 is required for furniture, fittings, initial marketing and other start-up costs. Leases for premises and for specialist equipment will cost a total of £20,000 a year. Other fixed costs will total £5,000 a year. Total labour costs are estimated at £125,000 in Year 1. At the projected level of sales, ingredients and consumables will cost another £30,000 in the first year and more as turnover grows in future.

Projected revenue of £192,000 in the first year is expected to be enough to break even after financing costs and allowing a margin of safety. The best available estimates for subsequent years are £230,000 in Year 2, £285,000 in year three and higher levels thereafter. The corresponding profit levels are £25,000 in year two and £60,000 in Year 3.

Initial cash requirements are included in the start-up capital. Once the business is operating, retail customers will pay cash (as is normal) while supplies will be bought with 50 days' trade credit. No cash flow difficulties are anticipated in this situation and projections suggest that the business can operate with no overdraft.

The basis for all the financial estimates is detailed in Appendix 3.

Finance

The partners will invest £60,000 of their own capital and seek to borrow another £40,000, repayable over 4 years. They are confident that this business will be profitable and will have no difficulty in making scheduled repayments.

Appendices

The appendices are not included in this unit guide but would be a vital part of a real plan. A bank or another potential lender would probably pay particularly close attention to the data in the appendices, most notably those supporting the profit estimates and the assertion on cash flow. Assuming that the appendices look convincing, the plan would give evidence for a decision on how risky and how profitable the business proposal seems.

Tasks

(1) What, in this business plan, would encourage a bank to make a loan?
(2) Make a list of five points that should encourage a bank to lend.
(3) Would you advise a bank to lend to Bradford Bakers' Café?
(4) Is there more information that you would want before giving advice?

Edexcel AS Business Studies/Economics & Business

Putting a business idea into practice

- Drawing up a business plan is a very sensible preparation for a new business. It is also essential before organisations such as banks will consider lending money.

- There is some variation in business plan contents but the name, product, personnel and financial estimates on costs, revenue and financing are included. Market research information is frequently a valuable component.

- Bank websites will often give advice on business plans and sometimes offer a preferred layout.

Summary

Questions & Answers

The exam

Assessment objectives

Exam candidates are tested through their demonstration of four skills known as assessment objectives (AOs). Marks for each question are either linked to one of the skills or more frequently shared between more than one of them — every mark awarded is for the use of a skill.

A question asking 'What is meant by...?' can just be testing knowledge, but few questions are that simple. The toolkit approach helps to explain the skills. It is useful if car mechanics understand what spanners are made of and how they work, it is more important that mechanics can use spanners and know when they have done their job properly. Our tools in this subject are the ideas and theories we use, the assessed skills focus on how well we understand and use them.

In order to answer a question such as 'Assess alternative ways of financing a new small hairdressing salon' you would be expected to know what sources of finance are possible, to look at how well each might fit to the needs of such a business and what problems they could generate, then to make a judgement on which type of financing might be best. Questions such as this combine all four of the assessed skills.

Knowledge and understanding (AO1)

The AO1 objective covers knowing and understanding the terms and subject content that make up our toolkit. Besides being able to define them, you must understand them and be able to explain how they are useful — which is not quite the same thing. For example, learning a definition of 'breakeven point' does not in itself mean that you really understand it, any more than learning a definition of spark plugs or disc brakes would help an apprentice mechanic to identify and fix a fault.

Application (AO2)

The exam questions come with information to describe a particular setting or context: for example, my question about new business finance used the context of hairdressing. Fitting subject ideas and theories to a context is called **application**. Questions often ask you to explain how concepts fit a context. Some harder questions, especially in later units, supply data on a problem in a context and leave you to choose which toolkit concepts to use. There might be hints in the data about possibilities.

When mechanics are told that a car is losing power, they will look for clues in the information given but need their skills and toolkit to identify and repair the fault. They will have ideas about common faults with cars and how to cure them; similarly, you will have developed experience by working on a variety of business problems.

Analysis (AO3)

Chemical analysis means breaking something down to identify its constituent parts. In Business and Economics we use toolkit concepts to get below the surface and build logical explanations. For example, we know that rises in interest rates tend to slow demand for businesses and to reduce economic growth. Just making the statement in the last sentence is an **assertion**, a claim with no evidence or logical reasoning to back it up. However, explaining how and why demand and growth slow would be **analysis**. Part of the answer here concerns a shift in expectations and optimism; there is also a 'monetary transmission mechanism', which is part of a more complex toolkit than we need for this unit.

Many students fail to earn analysis marks because they just make assertions — and there are no marks for assertion. If mechanics see that the level of a key fluid is low they might suspect a leak: finding the cause to explain the leak would be the mechanics' equivalent to our analysis. The need for logic in analysis underlines the importance of effective written communication. Analysis and evaluation marks will suffer if ideas are not expressed clearly. Link words that ties phrases together are important because they are a sign of logical analysis. 'Because' was a link word in the last sentence. So, if, unless, therefore and however are other common examples. Examiners sometimes look for use of link words as an indicator of analysis.

Evaluation (AO4)

We all make many decisions, ranging from everyday and trivial to life-changing ones. **Evaluation** is about using organised judgement to support decision making. If you develop strong evaluation skills you can expect to do well in this course and to strengthen an ability that employers prize and you will find invaluable at times throughout your life.

Building on toolkit ideas (of course) and the other skills, full evaluation entails looking at the strengths and weaknesses of a suggestion, or of alternatives, before reaching a supported judgement. A good comparison here is with a court of law — juries listen to the prosecution and defence evidence before weighing up the arguments to reach a judgement. The decision you reach in an evaluation will not be a right or wrong answer: it will be a good evaluation if it is based on a sound use of evidence and skills. To highlight the importance of clear written English, one evaluation question in the exam will be marked with an asterisk* and have the quality of written communication emphasised in the mark scheme.

In addition to full evaluation, there can be situations where brief statements that show judgement (or '**evaluative comments**') score evaluation marks.

The types of evaluative comment that can be rewarded in an appropriate context include:
- commenting on the importance of a point made
- identifying conditions necessary for a development
- judging the probability of a point
- distinguishing between short- and long-run consequences
- distinguishing between winners and losers
- distinguishing between personal and public interest
- assessing risks
- identifying significant specific additional information that would help

Table 3 Assessment objectives and weightings

AO1	Demonstrate knowledge and understanding of the specified content.	30%
AO2	Apply knowledge and understanding of the specified content to problems and issues arising from both familiar and unfamiliar situations.	30%
AO3	Analyse problems, issues and situations.	20%
AO4	Evaluate, distinguish between and assess appropriateness of fact and opinion, judge information from a variety of sources.	20%

Exam format

Unit 1 carries 50% of the AS marks, whichever second unit it is combined with. It also carries 25% of overall marks for students who take the full GCE A-level.

The exam for this unit lasts for 75 minutes and a total of 70 marks are available. Allowing 5 minutes for reading through the paper first, this means that you have 1 minute to earn each mark. You have no choice of questions. The structure of this unit is tied to the allocation of a total of 21 marks to rewarding knowledge and 21 for application; 14 marks are awarded for analysis and 14 for evaluation.

At the start of the exam booklet there are eight supported multiple-choice questions in Section A. In each case there is 1 mark for picking the right answer plus 3 additional marks for explaining why that is the correct answer. You can earn some marks by explaining why the other answers are wrong. It is difficult to test evaluation skills via multiple-choice questions, and most of the marks in this section will be for the 'lower' skills. Total marks for the multiple-choice questions are $8 \times 4 = 32$.

Section B provides a collection of data on a particular situation or context (often adapted newspaper articles plus perhaps tables or charts of data) and sets a 'structured' string of questions related to the context. Typically, there are one or two straightforward questions first, which carry only a few marks. There are more marks for later sections that concentrate on the higher skills of analysis and evaluation. With few marks for the higher skills in multiple-choice questions, it is inevitable that these higher skills will figure extensively in Section B.

Students who are strong on analysis and evaluation will score more marks on the structured data–response question and consequently have the best chance of reaching the top grades. The comments on the weaker answers given to the first sample question and the impressive answers to the second sample in the Questions and Answers section illustrate what good analysis and evaluation are. There are 38 marks available in Section B, and the minute-per-mark rule means that a 5-mark question should take only half the time used on a 10-mark question. Avoid the expensive mistake of running out of time before reaching the last section, which normally carries the largest allocation of marks. If time management could be a problem for you, plenty of practice in timed conditions should help. As a last resort, you might even decide not to leave the sections with most marks until last.

Tackling multiple-choice questions

How do you start?

Your first task with each of these questions is to pick the right answer from the four alternatives. The 'stem' statement at the start of the question normally points you to the right section of the specification and a few questions might just be checking on basic knowledge. There should be some questions where the answer is obvious. It is often possible to quickly rule out some answers that are irrelevant or plainly wrong, sometimes three of the four options. If you are stuck on a question, move on and return to it later. It will help your confidence to tackle some questions that you find relatively easy first. It is rare for sensibly prepared candidates to find all the multiple-choice questions in the paper difficult.

How to read the questions

The questions are not written to trick you but do need careful reading. Missing a word such as 'not' will obviously send you astray. 'Must' means something will always be the case, whereas 'can' just means that there is a possibility. Being careful about the use of words is nearly as important as understanding your subject toolkit. Good communication skills are about effective reading and careful understanding as well as writing. Practising at using words precisely develops a valuable skill.

> **Examiner tip**
> You must take real care reading the questions. Missing or misreading a word can easily lead you away from the right answer.

What do you do if you're stuck?

If you rule out two options but are clueless between the remaining two, *guess* as a last resort. Both leaving a question blank and getting an answer wrong score zero, so getting a question wrong is no worse than making no attempt. Guessing when stuck is sensible. If you correctly rule two options out, that leaves a 50% chance of a mark for guesswork. Some students use systems for guessing but I've never met a reliable one. For instance, one student had a theory that longer answers were often right, so went for the longest plausible answer when guessing — but right answers can be short. Of course, the more you understand the subject, the less you will need to guess.

What other marks are available?

Getting the multiple-choice answer right is actually less important than how you approach the other 3 marks on each question. You are required to explain *why* your answer is correct. Here, identifying and sometimes defining the most relevant toolkit item can often be a good start (see sample questions and answers on pp. 50–57). If you know a diagram that helps with the explanation, you can draw it (but remember that you have just 3 minutes for this type of answer). If you are a little uncertain on the explanation, there is generally 1 mark each available for explaining why a couple of the other options are wrong. Examiners normally have a list of points worth a mark each (or sometimes 2 marks for important points): your job is to earn 3 marks by hitting points on the list.

Scores achieved on multiple-choice sections vary widely. Students with the skills and enough experience to be comfortable with these questions will often score 30 or more of the 32 marks available. Some other candidates panic, leave blanks, guess wildly and score less than a random guesser might. Practice helps, so pester your teacher for plenty of examples. It takes a real effort, but working out where and why you have gone wrong on sample questions is a powerful way of learning and improving.

Tackling structured data–response questions

What are these questions testing?

Including data on specific business/economic contexts in the exam paper has a variety of purposes. First of all, it forces you to think for yourself and use the examined skills rather than repeat your notes. The application skill shows this clearly; if you fail to make any reference to the data context in your answers your marks will suffer. In a question about a sole trader, for example, it is useless to repeat your notes on shareholders and annual general meetings. Some weak students exasperate examiners by skipping through the data supplied and making no reference to it in their answers. The intention is that you should use your toolkit on the problems and situations specified.

How do you use the data in the question effectively?

Just as ignoring the data is wrong, it would be equally foolish to copy out large chunks of it. There are no marks for this. The sensible approach is to copy short quotes where you can pick out really important points and refer to the line numbers for chunks of data that you want to write about. For example, 'as explained in lines 7–10 of evidence B' would be perfectly acceptable.

Some students find it useful to underline key points in the evidence for data–response questions. This can be useful as your attention will be drawn back to these points as you think about your answers — as long as you can identify key points and don't underline too much. Examiners will not look at anything you write on the evidence pages, just at your answers.

How are the questions structured?

Data–response questions have a structured sequence of parts that generally build up through the skills and become more complex. A typical start could be an 'Identify' or 'What is meant by?' question that tests knowledge or/and application, carries just a few marks and is worth only 2 or 3 minutes of your time. Subsequent parts will build up to the higher skills, carry more marks and be worth spending more time on. Every question will have two or three evaluation sections. Thinking and planning before you start writing your answer will help you to gain more of the 10 or so marks available on the evaluation sections.

What skills ensure a good answer?

A good evaluation answer uses all four skills:

(1) You must build from a good grasp of the relevant toolkit.
(2) It is then important to write an answer that applies your toolkit convincingly to the data context.
(3) Explaining things rather than taking them for granted will earn analysis marks.
(4) Finally, you need to reach a judgement (evaluation) that is supported by what you have written.

What is the best approach to evaluation?

If you have a straightforward 'assess the merits' style of question, a three-stage approach works best:

(1) Identify and explain good points.
(2) Explore weaknesses.
(3) Finally, reach a judgement based on the points you think are most important.

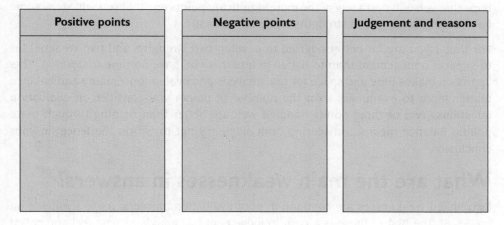

Figure 7 Three-box diagram approach

In developing this skill, it makes sense to start planning answers by jotting points in three boxes as shown in Figure 7. If you take a minute to jot points in this way in an exam, it will help you to structure your answer well.

Take as an example 'Assess the merits of running an independent business'. In the good points box I would put: 'being able to focus on what I enjoy most', 'having independence' and 'keeping any profit'. Negative points could be: 'an uneven income', 'having to find a market' and 'the need to organise carefully'. A good answer would include some toolkit points (e.g. about characteristics of entrepreneurs, market mapping and financing) and logical explanation rather than assertion. My own evaluation would be that it suits me to mix some work for other organisations with running an independent business part time. In other words, the merits of running an independent business are sufficient to have an appeal but not so strong that I choose to give up some work for other employers.

How many points should you make?

Your circumstances and *your* judgement will be different and this raises a really important point. There isn't just *one* right answer to evaluation questions. What matters is that the judgement you reach fits the points you have explored. Mark schemes allow high marks for positive *or* negative conclusions, as long as you see strengths and weaknesses and develop an answer using all the assessed skills. If you can add a little more sophistication by identifying conditions that your judgement depends on, or acknowledging that short-run consequences will be different from the long run (for example), your evaluation score will climb.

It can take a lifetime to reach a full evaluation of complex problems: judgement is a time-consuming process. You will have around 12 minutes for the evaluation parts of these questions.

Examiners know that you cannot do justice to every possible point. There is a danger here that can particularly damage the answers of conscientious students. If you think of and raise so many points that your time is swallowed up by listing them, you won't have time to develop the higher skills for which more marks are allocated. Examiners hope that you will find a few of the more significant points and that you will show some balance (e.g. some mix of strengths and weaknesses).

For Unit 1 you are far better advised to develop two strengths and two weaknesses to support a judgement than to list 20 points that you have no time to develop. This approach makes time and space for real analysis and evaluation. Quality and balance matter more to examiners than the number of points you consider on evaluation questions. Two or three points handled well are better than rushing through more points. Balance means considering both sides: try not to 'sit on the fence' in your conclusion.

What are the main weaknesses in answers?

Two linked weaknesses are common in poor evaluation answers. As you will see on pp. 58–61, the first of these is a rush to judgement by candidates who feel compelled to put a concluding assertion in the first sentence. Conclusions belong at the end and a relevant definition is often a better start. After starting with a sweeping assertion, it is then difficult to show balance. If, for example, an answer starts by claiming that a particular strategy is good, it then becomes difficult to see any weaknesses or downside. This is the second weakness. Examiners prefer answers that have enough balance to recognise strengths and weaknesses before settling on a conclusion. However good a strategy is, there are always likely to be risks and costs associated with it. Balance means considering weaknesses as well as strengths.

Overall, try to stick close to the minute per mark approach. As with multiple-choice questions, there is good evidence that practice improves performance on data-response. You will improve most if you try to learn from your own mistakes. Rather than just look at the marks on work that has been handed back by your teacher, and then forgetting it, think about where you missed marks and what you need to do to improve.

Command words

Each question contains an instruction relating to which assessed skills are to be used. The precise structure of the question leads to minor variations but the table below shows what common command words are looking for.

Command	Skills requirement
• Identify • List • Give one reason • Outline • What is meant by • State • How could	These are simple commands looking either for knowledge or knowledge plus application. Marks allocated to such questions will be low. The structure of AS papers means that they will be fairly scarce. They test assessment objectives AO1 or AO1 and AO2.
• Briefly explain • Explain • Analyse • Why might	Explanation is a key part of analysis (AO3) though these commands commonly also include the lower skills. The mark allocation often indicates depth of analysis required.
• Examine • Comment	These commands at least require analysis. When mark allocation is (say) 6 or more, an evaluative comment (AO4) will often also be wanted.
• Discuss	This word has a different meaning in exams from its everyday use. It requires balance and evaluation (AO4) as well as analysis and the lower skills.
• Assess • Critically examine • Evaluate • To what extent • Justify • Recommend	These are the main evaluation commands. If you offer no judgement or balance when any of these commands are used, you will not do well. Questions with these commands generally carry higher mark allocations. All four skills/assessment objectives are tested by these command words.

Sample questions

This section includes two sets of eight multiple-choice questions; the set of eight that you will meet in an exam should be written in a similar style. There are also two structured data–response questions, again written in the style that you will find in the question you meet in the exam. One development since the first exams is that evidence of students having to rush has led to some reduction in the number of parts in the data–response questions.

After each set of multiple-choice questions there is a set of specimen answers. You can earn the 3 explanation marks by giving a good account of why one answer is correct. Questions have an example or context that you can use in your explanation. Marks for a partial explanation can be boosted by explaining why other answers are wrong. This is illustrated in the specimens but is not necessary when explanations are good enough for the 3 marks. Spending too long on these answers has an opportunity cost of less time for structured data–response.

In the structured data–response questions given here, the command words are in italics to help you remember which skills are required. The sample responses to these questions take two approaches. The first question has typical grade-D responses overall, plus examiner comments and hints on how the answers could have been improved. Examiner comments on the answers are indicated by the icon ⓔ.

The second structured data–response question has grade-A* standard answers. The examiner's comments highlight the strengths of the responses. You are likely to learn more from these responses if you look at them and make comparisons only after you have written answers of your own.

Practice at answering questions provides valuable experience. It would be sensible to allow yourself half an hour for *each set* of multiple-choice questions and 40 minutes *each* for the structured data–response questions, to keep in mind the time available. This time split reflects the division between the 32 marks available for multiple choice and 38 for data–response. You can then compare your responses with the samples, looking at where and how you do better than the examples given on structured data–response and also at where you could improve your work. Paying attention to the examiner's comments will improve your chances of writing more effective answers in future.

Reading the advice on tackling questions given on pp. 45–46 will be useful, before you answer these questions. Looking at it again before your exam should be useful too.

Your exam paper takes the form of a booklet with answer spaces after each question. Answer spaces are not included in this guide. An exercise book or lined paper can be used for your answers.

Sample structured multiple-choice questions

Set 1

For each question below, the correct answer is awarded 1 mark. A valid explanation of why your answer is correct earns up to 3 marks.

(1) Ingvar Kamprad, of Ikea fame, was described as an autocratic leader. An advantage of working for an autocratic leader is that you:

A   are involved in decision-making

B   know that decisions will take your interests into account

C   are seldom left to make difficult decisions

D   will be punished for any indiscipline

(2) Some newspapers stay in business despite having little prospect of profit. Many entrepreneurs do NOT maximise profits because they:

A are invariably inefficient

B are willing to behave unethically

C operate in competitive industries

D prioritise objectives other than profit

(3) Even small businesses such as local hairdressers have fixed and variable costs. A distinction between fixed and variable costs is that:

A fixed costs are higher than variable costs

B fixed costs can never be changed

C variable costs are more predictable

D variable costs change with output

(4) The value of £1 against $1 fluctuates. A high rate of the pound sterling against the US dollar will:

A only affect people who travel abroad

B make UK exports less competitive in the USA

C make UK exports more competitive overseas

D have less impact if the pound is also high against the euro

(5) Starting a new business means becoming an entrepreneur. One thing that most entrepreneurs have in common is that they:

A take responsibility and some risk

B own successful businesses

C are autocratic leaders

D provide capital to finance their business

(6) Agencies such as Mintel often conduct primary market research. The distinction between primary and secondary market research is that:

A primary market research is conducted before a business begins operations

B primary market research is less complex

C secondary market research draws on information collected by others

D secondary market research follows up primary data

(7) A bank would expect to use a business plan in deciding whether to lend to a new business. A business plan:

A can only be written once a new business starts

B is likely to be modified once a business starts operation

C cannot predict profit or cash flow

D is a legal requirement for a new business

(8) The owner of a new clothes boutique might be well advised to use market mapping. Market mapping can help entrepreneurs to:

A identify a potential market niche

B see the competitive advantage of their product

C understand how they add value

D all of the above

Answers to Set I

Question I

Answer C

ⓔ An autocratic leader such as Ingvar Kamprad keeps power and major decision taking to himself/herself and is reluctant to delegate. This means that employees of autocratic leaders will normally be following orders rather than taking difficult decisions. This might not be an advantage if employees want responsibility but it is reasonable to assume that most people dislike making difficult decisions.

Answer A is wrong because decision taking is centred on the one autocrat. B might be true of a paternalistic leader but not necessarily of an autocrat. D might be true of an autocrat, but also true with other leadership, and in any case punishment is not an advantage.

NB If you have given a confident explanation of the right answer to this type of question, it is not essential to explain why the alternatives are wrong.

Question 2

Answer D

ⓔ Some newspapers want to promote views they support and accept losses. Similarly, if an entrepreneur prioritises independence or working for a comfortable number of hours, for example, he or she will not be maximising profits because other objectives have been given higher priority. It could be that expansion would increase profits but the entrepreneur prefers to keep a business small.

A is wrong because it uses the word 'invariably' so just one efficient entrepreneur would invalidate this statement. B is illogical because an entrepreneur tempted to unethical behaviour is likely to have been attracted by greater potential profits. Competitive pressure can force people to operate efficiently; this does not conflict with profit maximisation, so option C is wrong.

Question 3

Answer D

ⓔ The definition of variable costs is that they change with output, for example when a hairdresser needs more shampoo to wash more customers' hair. If variable costs did not change with output they would not vary.

A is tempting because fixed costs are often higher, but this is not always the case, so this answer is wrong. B is simply false. Fixed costs stay the same when output changes in the short run, but they can change in the long run. C is normally untrue: fixed costs are more predictable in the short run.

Question 4

Answer B

ⓔ A high pound against the dollar will increase the price of UK exports in the USA, making them less price competitive. More dollars will be needed to pay for any amount of pounds sterling to buy British exports.

A is wrong because of imports. People who have never travelled abroad buy imported goods, so a high pound will make some imports cheaper for them. C is the reverse of the truth. A fall in the value of the pound rather than a rise would make exports more competitive. D is wrong because a high value against the euro would also make exports less competitive in European countries. This would increase rather than reduce the impact of the high pound on exports.

Question 5
Answer A

ⓔ Entrepreneurs are business organisers who will all take at least some responsibility, and an element of risk is unavoidable in business. Taking responsibility and risk are key parts of being an entrepreneur

All entrepreneurs cannot be successful: some will fail, so B is wrong. Some entrepreneurs are democratic or *laissez-faire* leaders rather than autocratic. Thus answer C is simply wrong. They will not all finance their own businesses; most will borrow at least part of the capital used, so D is also wrong.

Question 6
Answer C

ⓔ Primary market research is new research carried out for the first time, often by agencies such as Mintel. Secondary research accesses information previously collected. Answer C is an accurate statement about secondary research.

A is wrong as established businesses carry out new research. B and D are both factually incorrect statements as primary research can be on complex qualitative matters and many businesses will first use secondary research.

Question 7
Answer B

ⓔ A business plan depends on estimates and future events in its construction. B makes sense as estimates used in planning are unlikely to prove completely accurate, therefore it is best to modify the plan once real data is available. This is the correct answer.

Business plans are best written before operations start, so A is wrong. Estimates or predictions of cash flow and profits might not be accurate but they are an important element of a business plan, making C inaccurate. D is wrong as business plans are not a legal requirement.

Question 8
Answer D

ⓔ A market map, which plots brands against two major variable features of a product, can show gaps in the market that are neglected niches. This could be very valuable to a new boutique. It can also show how brands are differentiated, which can be a source of competitive advantage. This can also shed light on how a brand adds value. Thus, A, B and C are all plausible. As the stem says 'can' rather than 'must', this makes D correct.

Set 2

For each question below, the correct answer is awarded 1 mark. A valid explanation of why your answer is correct earns up to 3 marks.

(1) Online music retailers can cater for 'the long tail'. In such a context the 'long tail' refers to:
- A backlogs of unpaid invoices damaging small business cash flow
- B the time lags involved in launching a new business
- C appendices attached to business plans
- D increasing scope for development of specialist niche markets

(2) Unemployment in some UK areas is double the national average. The impact of high local unemployment on a firm will be:
- A bad if the firm wants to recruit workers
- B bad if the product is a luxury sold locally
- C good if the firm only uses skilled workers
- D good if the product is an exported inferior good

(3) Electrician Steve has decided to use cost-plus pricing in his new business. Cost-plus pricing:
- A guarantees that a business will be profitable
- B is based on what the market will pay
- C entails calculating likely cost and pricing to include a profit
- D depends on prices set by rival firms

(4) Global demand for netbooks has risen. A demand curve will shift to the right if:
- A the product becomes more fashionable
- B the price of the product falls
- C supply of the product increases
- D costs of production increase

(5) Theo Paphitis is a venture capitalist. A venture capitalist is:
- A an entrepreneur who starts new businesses
- B a long-established business leader
- C a specialist at financing new or expanding businesses
- D an entrepreneur whose business fails

(6) The market for footwear is segmented. Market segmentation entails:
- A splitting a global market into geographical regions
- B firms agreeing to share a market between them
- C dividing up the physical locations of a market
- D splitting consumers into groups with distinct preferences

(7) Any new business is well advised to draw up a business plan. A business plan will generally include:
- A cost, revenue and profit estimates
- B expected cash-flow data
- C market research information
- D all of the above

(8) Many market research firms are market oriented. Market orientation necessarily entails:
- A outsourcing
- B demand-based pricing
- C prioritising customer requirements
- D all of the above

Answers to Set 2

Question 1

Answer D

e Chris Anderson's book *The Long Tail* focuses on the way in which computer and internet technology make it easier for firms such as online music sellers to cater for small, specialist niche markets that might previously have been ignored, so D is the correct answer. Specialist niches that were previously neglected can now be catered for.

Answers A and B refer to realistic problems facing new businesses but neither of these problems is associated with the name 'long tail'. Answer C simply identifies the fact that business plans tend to have appendices, but once again 'long tail' is irrelevant.

Question 2

Answer B

e High local unemployment might increase the availability of labour and might also depress local demand since unemployment tends to be associated with lower income. Luxury goods are likely to see a bigger reduction in sales than necessities when income falls. These points make B the correct answer because demand for a luxury sold locally can be expected to fall in an area when unemployment rises.

Answer A is wrong as local unemployment should make it easier to recruit. We have no information on the skills of unemployed workers, so cannot be sure about C. If the product is exported, the high local unemployment specified in D is irrelevant.

Question 3

Answer C

e Cost-plus pricing is based on estimation of cost and addition of a profit margin, as specified in answer C. This would be fairly easy for Steve to use.

Answer A is incorrect because setting a price does not in itself guarantee that sales will be sufficient to break even and reach profitability. Answer B refers to demand-based rather than cost-plus pricing. Answer D refers to price leadership or competitive pricing rather than the cost-plus pricing specified in the question.

Question 4

Answer A

 A change in any factor influencing demand, other than price, will lead to a shift in the demand curve. A shift to the right represents an increase in demand and this is to be expected when a product such as netbooks becomes more fashionable: A is correct.

Either a fall in price or an increase in supply will lead to a movement along the same demand curve rather than a shift to a new one, so B and C are wrong. Changes in costs will shift the supply curve rather than the demand curve so answer D is wrong.

Question 5

Answer C

 Venture capitalists specialise in the relatively high risk business of financing business start-ups, buyouts and expansions. They make funds available either as loans or in return for a share of ownership. They spread risks by being involved in a number of businesses at the same time. This description fits Theo and the correct answer, C.

Entrepreneurs start all types of business, mostly not connected to venture capital, so A is wrong. B and D also lack focus on the financing component that is central to venture capitalists, so they are wrong.

Question 6

Answer D

 Segmentation starts with identifying groups of consumers who share a set of preferences or characteristics, as described in D. A business can then tailor a product to fit such preferences. Tastes in footwear vary widely between groups.

Segmentation is not normally about geographical regions or physical locations, ruling out answers A and C. Answer B is about restrictive practices or a cartel, something quite different from segmentation.

Question 7

Answer D

 A business plan is a way of organising thinking and planning, which is important if a new business is to succeed. Completing a plan ensures that matters such as supply of materials to the business, financial estimates, human resources and a marketing plan have been thought through. A plan can be expected to include financial estimates on cash flow, revenue and profits plus relevant market research data. Thus, answer D is correct. Any of the other answers is too narrow, focusing on only part of a business plan.

Question 8

Answer C

 Market-orientated firms often do outsource production and focus mainly on marketing. It is also quite common for them to use demand-based pricing, starting from what their customers are willing to pay rather than, say, costs. The key to this question, though, is the word 'necessarily'

— because things are common they are not inevitably necessary. Some market-orientated firms produce their own goods and some use alternative approaches to pricing. C is correct as it identifies the essence of market orientation: it necessarily prioritises customer requirements rather than, say, the quality of the product, which is more central to product orientation. Market research firms are mostly market oriented.

Structured data–response questions

Question 1

Evidence A

Harold loves the Caribbean island where he lives and has no wish to move elsewhere. His biggest problem is that all the best jobs and careers on the island go to people who paid more attention to schoolwork then he ever did. He currently has a series of temporary and part-time jobs. The one he enjoys most is working as a driver/guide for a local minibus operator, taking trips for passengers from the cruise ships that call regularly at the island. He is paid $30 for guiding 4-hour trips that normally include a rainforest walk and visits to attractions such as waterfalls and an old fort. On a good day, tips can double his pay but his passengers don't always think of tipping.

Chatting to some passengers one day, Harold learns that they have paid the cruise ship operator $60 each for the excursion with him. In total, the ten of them have paid $600. This starts Harold thinking. When he takes the minibus back to the depot, Harold's boss tells him that the cruise operator pays him $150 per minibus and driver, but the contract specifies that he must have 12 minibuses available, even when only three or four are sometimes used and paid for.

A few people with taxis or old minibuses wait at the dockside and sometimes tempt tourists who have not booked trips from the cruise ship to take a cheaper excursion with them. Harold thinks that he could organise a tempting display of photographs, wear a smart uniform and present a more organised and attractive option. He can hire a minibus for $50 a day. If he charged $30 each and got three or more passengers (which seems easy) he could earn more than his present basic income from a day as driver/guide. With six passengers, he feels that he could organise a better tour than the present one, give his customers an enjoyable day and make more money for himself.

Evidence B

Table 1 Cruise ship visits to the island

	Sun	Mon	Tues	Weds	Thurs	Fri	Sat
High season	1	1	2	1	2	2	0
Low season	1	0	1	0	1	1	0

(a) (i) Using information in evidence **A,** *calculate* the gross profit ratio made by cruise ships on excursions sold to groups of ten customers. (2 marks)

ⓔ With a calculation always show your workings. They can score something even if your answer is wrong.

(ii) *Briefly explain* the difference between the calculated ratio and that of a typical business. (4 marks)

ⓔ Two steps here, first identify the difference, then explain it.

(b) *Examine* reasons why any two pieces of market research could be useful for Harold. (6 marks)

ⓔ Go beyond explanation to comment on your reasons here.

(c) *Assess* two potential sources of competitive advantage for Harold. (8 marks)

ⓔ Identify, explain, then make a judgement (e.g. how important, how easy to develop, which matters most?).

(d) *Assess* the case for Harold buying his own minibus if his business succeeds. (8 marks)

ⓔ Three steps: case for, case against, then weigh up in concluding judgement.

(e) *Evaluate* the strengths and weaknesses of Harold's proposed business.* (10 marks)

ⓔ As above, strengths then weaknesses, then your judgement (perhaps whether to proceed and why, or what to prioritise in starting up).

Student answers

(a) (i) If the ten people have paid $600 and the cruise operator has $150 as cost of sales, gross profit will be $450.

ⓔ **1/2 marks awarded** A decent start but a basic blunder. The candidate has not answered the question as there is no mention of 'ratio'. As the workings are on the right lines, most mark schemes would award 1 out of 2 marks.

(ii) This is a large profit in relation to the cost of sales and is much more than most businesses would expect **a**. Holidaymakers probably trust the cruise operator **b** and are afraid that a casually booked driver or minibus might be unsafe or unreliable, so they don't take the risk.

ⓔ **2/4 marks awarded** This reads plausibly enough but there are two problems with it. **a** There is no attempt to justify the assertion in the first sentence. **b** The second sentence relies on common sense rather than business and economics. It would have been easy to bring in toolkit concepts such as unique selling point or competitive advantage in explaining why the cruise operator can achieve such a margin. Alternatively, overheads could have been considered, such as the cost of marketing excursions and the wages of staff who process the bookings.

(b) On the days when there are cruise ships but Harold is not working, he could do useful market research at the dockside. Finding out how many holidaymakers take excursions with the local operators a and how many of the operators do and don't find customers would enable him to estimate how many potential customers there are. At the same time he could watch closely to see what works when the operators try to attract custom. He could learn a great deal about the market size and what gives competitive advantage. If most of the operators fail to attract custom, there would seem to be serious problems with his business proposal.

As a simple piece of secondary research b, he could study the harbour bookings data given in evidence B. This will quickly tell him that Saturday is the best choice for a day off. It also shows that there are potential customers 6 days a week c in the high season (double numbers on 3 days) but just 4 days a week in the low season, when boats could be less full too. Will he need to make extra profit in the high season in order to survive the low season?

ⓔ **6/6 marks awarded a** The student understands what market research is. **b** He even throws in identification of secondary research. Application to the context is spot on. There is some analytical development on both the research suggestions. **c** There is even good use of Evidence B.

(c) Harold's idea of dressing smartly and displaying photographs would give him competitive advantage over the local rivals at the dockside a. People are far more likely to choose someone who looks organised and smart as this suggests a responsible business. If Harold can make sure that his minibus looks clean and new, that would give competitive advantage as well. Compared to the cruise operator Harold has several disadvantages d but his main advantage in this case is price: he intends to charge half as much as the cruise operator does. This is a big price difference which will attract many holidaymakers. It is even likely that some people who have booked with the cruise operator would prefer to change to Harold although it is unlikely that they can get their money back from their first booking. As he is an experienced driver/guide, b this could be another source of competitive advantage if customers know about it.

ⓔ **4/8 marks awarded a** This candidate has shown a grasp of competitive advantage and identified some sound examples (= application). **b** The question specifies 'two' but the answer has more. The last sentence doesn't quite work but could be modified into projecting enthusiasm for the island. **c** The blunder this time is a failure to deal with the command word and required skills. 'Assess' calls for evaluation; what we have here is knowledge, application and some analysis. At a stretch, awareness of disadvantages in relation to the cruise d operator hints at some potential evaluation but this is not developed. In questions such as this 4 of the 8 marks are typically reserved for evaluation, restricting this candidate to 4/8.

(d) Buying his own minibus is a good idea a once he can afford it, because while he hires one he is paying a profit to someone else. Having a minibus that belongs to the business is bound to be cheaper. It means that he will only have to pay the costs b and not a profit to another owner.

A second benefit from owning the minibus is that it can become a marketing tool with the business name and attractive artwork. He can also

keep it spotlessly clean in order to impress potential customers. If he just rents minibuses by the day, he cannot personalise them to the business. **c**

The minibus will also become an asset **d** for the business. If he needs to raise cash in future or wants to close the business, he can sell it. He might even save tax **e** by buying the minibus as a business cost and also take advantage of it for his private use.

Harold should definitely **f** buy a minibus when the business can afford it.

ⓔ 3/8 marks awarded a The student has rushed to judgement in the first line and then focused only on trying to justify the hasty starting assertion. The points made in favour all have some merit. **e** The answer is totally unbalanced. An 'assess' question calls for a look at both sides to inform the conclusion (best reached at the end). This approach signals likely loss of all evaluation marks in line 1. **b** The first paragraph of this response is highly dubious. Harold will still need to pay a garage to maintain the minibus. It is quite possible that the hiring business can buy minibuses far cheaper than Harold and if they are efficient their prices for daily hire could be cheaper than the costs of owning and maintaining. If 'bound to be' had been replaced by possibly or probably the paragraph would have had more merit. **c** The second paragraph contains a useful idea with just a little development, i.e. application and perhaps 1 analysis mark. **d** The start of the third paragraph ignores the fact that, as Harold will have to pay for the minibus, it will have an opportunity cost. **e** There might be something in the point about tax. **f** To do better, this answer needs to look at the negative side of owning a minibus as well (e.g. opportunity cost, need to maintain and protect), preferably before reaching a judgement.

(e) Harold is a dreamer **a** with no realistic chance of turning his dreams into a business. Just as he went through school without achieving much, he has not thought through his ideas and they will not work.

He plans to spend money on the new clothes, photographs and mounting a display, hire a minibus for $50 and then hang about on the dockside **b** hoping that tourists will pay him for an excursion. Even assuming that he raises the money for these expenses **c**, he is unlikely to get it back.

Cruise ship passengers who want an excursion will book it on the ship rather than take a chance on an unknown individual who might put them in danger or rip them off **b**. If a few of them do take a chance on a local excursion, there are other, experienced, people with more knowledge of how to attract them. The high season might last for only a few weeks, perhaps school summer holidays but we are not told about this, and less than half as many ships call at the island for the rest of the year. This reduces his chances of finding enough customers even further.

Income distribution around the world is becoming less even with a bigger division between the 'haves' and the 'have-nots'. Harold is almost certainly a 'have-not' and a loser **b**. He is not the kind of person to successfully run a business.

ⓔ 3/12 marks awarded a Here we go again with a rush to judgement and a lack of balance. The student seems to have thrown out what his course has taught him and hurried a response with limited evidence of skills. This is not unusual for the last question on a paper. **b** He/she has plucked a few ideas from the evidence but combined them with inappropriate assertions and language such as 'hang about on the dockside', 'rip them off' and 'loser'. The asterisk against this question means that quality of written English is considered here, which makes the use of terms such as 'loser' unfortunate, though the use of sentences and fairly clear meaning are sound.

c The student shows some vague awareness of ideas like costs, but there is little evidence that he/she has mastered jargon and a toolkit. There is no sign of balance. The assertions are not real evaluation.

Overall, this candidate has scored 19/38. If he is also around half marks on the multiple-choice questions, his total will probably be enough for a grade D pass. The good news is that it is easy to avoid some of these blunders and improve on this mark. This shows that it is really not difficult to pass comfortably. It is even possible to make a few blunders and still reach a top grade. Only if you throw away evaluation marks as consistently as in this example, or if you miss whole questions out, will you struggle to pass.

Question 2

Evidence

Elaine went to college as an art student with a special interest in sculpture and soon found that what pleased her most was working with woods such as oak and elm. When she decided to make a coffee table, it surprised her that modern machinery in the college made light work of the basic preparation and allowed her to focus on detail and design quirks, which made her work unique. One of her senior lecturers bought the coffee table and suggested that Elaine's talent could be best employed in a business making furniture.

After various experiments, Elaine settled on dining tables with sets of chairs, each table to reflect Elaine's style and flair with her signature details plus some individuality. College staff, family and friends all thought that demand for the products would be strong.

Her research showed that renting an adequate workshop would cost £450 per month, including power, plus a £2,000 deposit returnable at the end of the lease. A 'wage' of £600 per month would be necessary to feed and keep her. Good quality wood would cost her £300 per set of table and chairs. It would also be necessary to rent a van for collection of materials and delivery of her products at a cost of £150 per month.

At a maximum, it would be possible for her to build six tables (with chairs) per month. There were two obvious possibilities for distribution. A large and prestigious department store offered to display a couple of her tables and might charge customers £1,100 from which it would keep £300 per sale. The alternative of starting an eBay shop on the internet might fetch an average of £900.

Elaine's intention was to build six tables before selling any, then to sell both ready-made sets and personalised tables and chairs made to order. Finishing her college course in debt meant that she had no money of her own to start a business. Her family were willing to lend her £2,000.

(a) (i) *Calculate* **Elaine's breakeven monthly sales if products are sold on eBay, showing your workings.**

(2 marks)

e This time there is an instruction to show workings – but always show them anyway.

(ii) *Briefly comment* **on the significance of this calculation.** (4 marks)

ⓔ Significance must be what this figure implies about the prospects of the business.

(b) *Explain* **why it is likely to be useful for Elaine to prepare a business plan.** (6 marks)

ⓔ 6 marks will want more than one reason, plus explanations for each.

(c) *Briefly assess* **the impact on Elaine's business of a rise in interest rates.** (6 marks)

ⓔ 'Assess' for just 6 marks, so a positive point, a negative point and then some judgement.

(d) *Assess* **the alternative channels of distribution that are suggested in the evidence.** (10 marks)

ⓔ 'Alternative' suggests the simplest evaluation is a comparison: which is better?

(e) *Evaluate* **two ways in which Elaine could increase revenue and profits once her business is established.** (10 marks)

ⓔ You have to think up two ways, preferably two ways that you can analyse then compare the merits of.

Student answers

(a) (i) The evidence specifies fixed monthly costs of £450 + £600 + £150 for the workshop, wages and van rental. Total fixed costs are £1,200 per month.
   The direct cost is £300 for wood so each table sold on eBay at £900 makes a contribution of £600 **a**. This means that just two tables will be the breakeven level of sales **b** as total revenue will then equal total costs.

ⓔ **2/2 marks awarded a** With only 2 marks for this question, spending too long on it would have an opportunity cost later in the exam. The calculations here are simple and accurate. **b** The answer avoids the trap of specifying breakeven in money terms, correctly identifying that it refers to a level of sales.

(ii) The calculation suggests that if Elaine sells three or more tables per month her business will be profitable. **a** With just two sales there would be no losses. This paints an optimistic picture **b** about the prospects of the business, especially as its capacity is six units per month. However, with no market research we cannot tell if the tables will be popular and sell, even though the department store was sufficiently interested to offer to stock them. **c**

ⓔ **4/4 marks awarded a** A good start that sets the scene clearly. In the worst situations, breakeven analysis can show that a business will struggle to be profitable, even when working close to capacity. **b** 'An optimistic picture' is an appropriate comment here. **c** The answer sensibly also notes that information on demand would also be needed to be completely confident about profitability.

(b) It is clear from the evidence that Elaine will not have sufficient assets of her own to provide capital for the business. Even if her family lend her £2,000 to cover the workshop deposit, her plan to build six table and chair sets before selling any will entail costs of at least £3,000 (£1,200 fixed costs + £1,800 for wood), before any revenue is received. In the almost certain event that Elaine needs to borrow money, a bank or many other lenders would want to see a business plan before seriously considering making a loan. **a**

Without constructing a business plan, Elaine might not even know how much borrowing is necessary. A well-constructed plan should give Elaine **b** valuable planning information and a way of judging how successful her business is as plans are overtaken by reality. It would be the business plan, for example, **c** that would clarify the cash-flow position and suggest how much to borrow.

Constructing a business plan can be time consuming and difficult but it forces would-be entrepreneurs to face up to essential questions about starting and operating the business. Elaine, like many others, is likely to find a business plan valuable, not just useful.

🅔 **6/6 marks awarded a** Stronger candidates would offer analysis of the need to borrow, as is seen here, whereas weaker candidates might simply assert that borrowing will be necessary. **b** Other than in the context of borrowing, this answer has generalisations about 'valuable planning information' and 'face up to essential questions' but is a little short on specifics. **c** 'Clarify the cash flow and suggest how much to borrow' is clear and good. Positive marking should just bring this answer 6/6.

(c) Those businesses that are cash rich gain from an interest rate increase, as their bank deposits earn more interest. Initially, it seems that Elaine's business will be borrowing and, if her borrowing is an overdraft or a loan with variable interest, her interest payments will increase. In effect her costs will rise, so profits will fall. Many dining tables are bought as replacements when people decide to 'trade up'. This is discretionary spending that could be discouraged when the cost of borrowing increases, especially if consumer confidence weakens at the same time. Such a fall in confidence is one possible consequence of an interest rate increase.

If we think of this in terms of supply and demand, rising costs could push the supply curve up and left, while falling confidence and rising borrowing costs push the demand curve down and left. A reduction in the quantity sold seems inevitable. **a**

The extent of these negative effects depends heavily on the extent of the interest rate rise. In recent years the Bank of England has changed its base rate by 0.25% at a time. One small increase is unlikely to have a major impact. It is also probable that an interest rate increase would be intended to counter inflationary pressure. In other words, its aim could be to stop the economy from overheating. If this is the case and demand might have been high in the economy, it might still be reasonable after a small interest rate change. **b**

The relative significance of extra interest charges would be small if Elaine's borrowings are limited. The bigger danger to her business is probably the risk of a downturn in demand as furniture sales are influenced by consumer confidence. **c**

🅔 **6/6 marks awarded** The 'assess' command here calls for evaluation or judgement. In this case, judging whether an interest rate rise is good or bad for the business, as at **a** seems too simple. **b** The strength of this answer is that it focuses on the extent of likely negative consequences. The argument that a small rise in interest rates might have little impact shows good judgement. **c** The conclusion that the impact on demand is likely to be a bigger danger than the impact on costs is also sound evaluation. Few answers would be better than this.

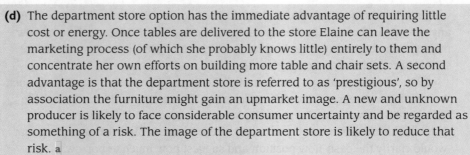

(d) The department store option has the immediate advantage of requiring little cost or energy. Once tables are delivered to the store Elaine can leave the marketing process (of which she probably knows little) entirely to them and concentrate her own efforts on building more table and chair sets. A second advantage is that the department store is referred to as 'prestigious', so by association the furniture might gain an upmarket image. A new and unknown producer is likely to face considerable consumer uncertainty and be regarded as something of a risk. The image of the department store is likely to reduce that risk. **a**

The obvious disadvantage of the department store is that it would take £300 of the revenue generated by each set. This would leave Elaine with only £800 per set, not the £1,100 charged or the £900 that eBay sales could generate. This is a reduction in revenue per set sold and possibly in the profits of the business. Elaine would also have to be careful to get an agreement on how quickly the store would hand over revenue due to her. If the store management are slow payers, that could cause her cash-flow problems. It is also possible that the approach the store takes to the furniture and the way it tries to sell it might not fit with Elaine's preferences. **b**

Elaine would keep control if her own website was used and be able to keep the style of the website consistent with the style of the furniture. It might also be easier to keep direct contact with customers and understand their preferences, should a website be used. If the estimate in the evidence is correct, each set sold by the website would generate £100 more revenue than the store so there would be more profit on each set. **a**

There is nothing in the evidence suggesting that Elaine has IT skills, if she has to pay someone else to construct and operate the website that will bring an additional cost. If, alternatively, she builds her own website, this might prove harder than expected and would certainly have an opportunity cost in terms of time and energy. Just constructing a website does not guarantee that people wanting tables will find it. It would be necessary to advertise and seek publicity about the website's existence. **b**

Both of these approaches have their strengths and weaknesses. Using the department store is simpler, would certainly be a less complicated way to start and would ensure that some people see the furniture. This seems a better first choice. **c** There is nothing to stop Elaine from also starting a website if she wants more business from a wider market once some sales have been generated by the department store, so there is a case for using both channels of distribution together. **d**

ⓔ 10/10 marks awarded This answer takes the classic three-box approach to evaluation, which examiners hope for and reward but see less often than they should. **a** It starts by identifying strengths and **b** weaknesses of using the department store, moves on to strengths and weaknesses of a website and then **c** draws clear conclusions from the points made. **d** While many candidates would interpret this question as wanting a choice between the two options, it is legitimate to combine both as this would be feasible in the context. It is also possible that in other contexts strong candidates might reject both options and argue that a third choice of their own is better.

(e) Revenue measures the quantity sold multiplied by the unit price. If revenue is to increase, the business must either sell more tables or sell at a higher price. **a**

    The evidence suggests that Elaine is initially working alone. This means that some of her time is spent collecting wood and making deliveries. **b** Employing someone else to drive the van and take on other aspects of the work that are less skilled would enable Elaine to produce more furniture. Her initial limit of six sets per month might be increased to eight or even ten sets if someone else is working with her. This would be an attractive option if her output has previously been unable to keep up with demand, as the extra cost of one employee is unlikely to be as much as the extra revenue generated in this situation, so profits will rise. **d**

    Taking on an employee involves costs and risks in addition to the immediate wage. There are regulations and paperwork associated with employing anyone, national insurance and income tax for example. It is also unlikely that anyone new will have as much commitment to the business as Elaine. If her employee is chosen unwisely, there could be problems of unreliability and poorly completed tasks. This risk is greater as Elaine presumably has no previous experience as an employer. There is also the possibility that in order to sell more, Elaine will have to reduce the price of her furniture. If the price is reduced too much, profit could actually fall. Employing someone and increasing output brings risks.

    e If demand is healthy, another route to extra revenue and profits might be to simply increase the price. **c** If, say, there were ten people wanting her furniture each month but only six sets available, **d** a price increase could easily still allow her to sell the six sets. This obviously depends on how much the price is increased and how big an increase it takes to put off potential buyers. If the tables are seen as exclusive, high quality and a status symbol, it is possible that Elaine could decide on a substantial price increase.

    It is hard for Elaine to know how customers will react to a price change. There is a risk that any price increase will put them off and lead to reduced sales and revenue. It would be sensible to undertake some market research before raising the price. If sales are made by the department store, it would be necessary for them to accept the price increase too. **e**

    The price increase would be the quicker and easier option, especially as price could be brought back down if the increase brought problems. **f** This is probably the better short-run choice. For the longer term it is important to **g** consider Elaine's objectives and priorities. Expansion would get her business known more widely, which could bring long-run benefits. Focusing on the creative part of the business and delegating other tasks to an employee might be attractive. Alternatively, there could be gains from taking on a trainee capable of sharing her enthusiasm and contributing creative ideas to the business in future. If such possibilities are attractive to Elaine, expansion is the better long-term option. However, if she values her independence and wants to keep control over everything that happens, staying small and raising price is the better choice.

ⓔ 10/10 marks awarded This answer has many of the features of the best evaluation. **a** Starting with a relevant toolkit definition is often a good idea and here it is linked well to a next sentence that sets the scene for development. **b,c** There are two clear and contrasting alternatives on how to raise revenue. **d,e** Strengths and weaknesses of both are considered. **f** The concluding section is relatively sophisticated. **g** Rather than simply choosing one option, it identifies the considerations to be taken into account when a choice is made. At the same time, this is not a 'sitting on the fence' answer that is reluctant to reach a judgement. It is easy to give this response all the available marks.

(e) **38/38 marks awarded** An answer such as this, which drops no marks on an entire structured data–response question, is rare. This is the type of work that will earn the A* grade if it is coupled with sound multiple-choice answers and continued at A2.

Knowledge check answers

1 Taking some chances is an inevitable part of running a business and risk-averse people would be reluctant to do this. This makes them unlikely to be good entrepreneurs, though excessive risk taking is also potentially disastrous.

2 They might be relaxed about such things as the marks they earn, doing enough to stay out of trouble (or out of too much trouble) but not spending time on tasks such as studying ways they could improve their performance.

3 In fast food, McDonald's and Burger King are obvious example. Adidas and Nike might quickly come to mind for sports shoes. Oil giants such as Exxon (Esso) are in most countries. A full list is difficult as more multinationals are expanding and trying to become global.

4 Primary research is new information gathered for the first time, secondary means making use of existing data.

5 Segmentation by age group is obvious, e.g. baby clothes. Work clothing (and uniform) is a segment. Fashionable clothing could be a third example but many other segments could be identified.

6 Two reasons are plausible here. First, price cutting can be a competitive strategy, aimed at increasing market share by attracting more customers and perhaps also at making life difficult for rivals. Second, a struggling business might have no choices other than to cut prices to stay in business or to close down.

7 • Segments tend to be bigger; niches are often more narrowly defined.
   • Market orientation means prioritising what consumers want whereas positioning is choosing a combination of qualities for a brand, e.g. cheap and colourful.

   • Stakeholders are any groups with an interest in a business; shareholders are the owners of a company.
   • Opportunity cost is the best alternative given up when a choice is made; money cost refers only to cash paid.

8 Lower interest rates reduce the cost of borrowing, perhaps tempting consumers to spend and making business more willing to borrow.

9 Their commitment to study means students are not available for full-time work.

10 • income tax — cut so people have more to spend
   • government spending — raised to increase incomes and spending
   • interest rates — down to encourage spending rather than saving
   • exchange rate of the pound — down to make UK businesses more competitive

11 Profit is revenue minus costs whereas cash flow measures incoming payments over time and spending.

12 Variable costs change whenever output does; fixed costs can only be varied in a longer time period.

13 If spending exceeds receipts, the business might become unable to make due payments on time. This could lead to failure of the business.

14 It lets them form an opinion on the chances of getting back any money they lend, and also shows that the people involved are organised.

15 'Flexibility' suggests some element of variable cost, especially with part-time and seasonal staff. If others are paid overtime, this is a variable cost too.

Page numbers in **bold** refer to key term definitions